THE EMBA

C000253983

THE EMBATTLED CHRISTIAN

*William Gurnall
and the Puritan View
of Spiritual Warfare*

BRYAN G. ZACHARIAS

THE BANNER OF TRUTH TRUST
1995

THE BANNER OF TRUTH TRUST
3 Murrayfield Road, Edinburgh EH12 6EL
P.O Box 621, Carlisle, Pennsylvania 17013, U.S.A.

© Bryan G. Zacharias 1995
First published 1995
ISBN 0 85151 675 0

Typeset in 10½ on 13 pt Garamond
by Watermark, Norwich

Printed and bound in Finland by WSOY

To my wife, Judy, and
our children Brandon, Rachel,
Judah, and Yaysha;

and

To my parents, Victor and
Marilouise Zacharias; my
brothers, Mark and Scott,
and their families;
and my sister Miriam

Contents

Abbreviation

The text used of William Gurnall's *Christian in Complete Armour* is that of the two-volume edition (Glasgow: William Blackie, 1864; repr., London: Banner of Truth, 1964) and quotations from this source will be identified simply by the volume number in roman numeral I or II, and page number. For example, (I:172), (II:356). Although the current Banner of Truth reprint of Gurnall is in one volume it retains the pagination of the two volumes.

Acknowledgements

This book was originally prepared as a thesis for the degree of Master of Christian Studies at Regent College, Vancouver. My first grateful acknowledgement must be to Dr. James I. Packer, my supervisor, whose example as a Christian man has been an inspiration to me. The seed idea for this thesis came from one of Dr. Packer's classes several years ago. I am grateful for his patience in waiting for this thesis to be completed, and for his very helpful comments and suggestions which helped clarify my thinking and expression.

Thanks are due also to Dr. Donald M. and Lindi Lewis, who led the thesis seminar, and to Dr. Lewis for his willingness to be my second reader.

To my beloved wife Judy, and to our children Brandon, Rachel, and Austin-Judah, I owe more than I can ever express. They have filled the years of my studies with years of joy, steadfast love, forgiveness, prayer, and support. For all Judy's patience which made this study possible, I shall be ever thankful.

I owe a great debt of love and gratitude to my parents, Victor and Marilouise Zacharias, whose legacy of Christian love and devotion has been of such blessing to me (and my wife and children). Little did they know in the years when they read Scripture and *Little Pilgrim's Progress* to me and my siblings, Mark, Scott, and Miriam, that those readings would eventually make their way into these pages. I thank them for both spiritual and very tangible material support during these years.

Grateful acknowledgement to Philip and Mandy O'Donoghue and their daughters for their loving friendship, prayers, and much assistance during some difficult times.

Thanks to John and Lorene Bowman for their friendship over many years (John always hoped I would be able to attend Regent College). I shall not forget how they drove hundreds of miles to loan me the computer which enabled me to get my first draft processed.

Many thanks to Carol Sinclair, my cousin, and her husband Rob, for their love, and their generous loan of another computer which enabled me to complete the task.

Thanks to Elie and Judith Nessim and Zion Messianic Fellowship; to Larry Stevens for his special help; to Pastor John and Michelle Opmeer and their family, Al and Sandra Robertson, and other friends from our years at Hope Reformed Church; to the Filipino fellowship; to my long-time friends Paul and Janet Gordon (Puritan lovers) and Michael Hammett from army days; and to many other relatives and friends.

Above all, 'thanks be to God, which giveth us the victory through our Lord Jesus Christ' (1 Corinthians 15:57).

BRYAN G. ZACHARIAS
JANUARY, 1995

1

Introduction

Western society has in recent years begun to manifest great interest and concern over 'spiritual' matters. Despite the dominance of naturalistic scientism for a time after Darwin, and the idea amongst some in the academic/scientific élite that such a view would effectively doom religion, recent events have shown the naïveté of such a belief. Communism, driven as it was by a so-called 'scientific' and atheistic worldview, in its recent collapse is only one of the more spectacular manifestations. The growth of Eastern mysticism and occultism in the West, in the popular and growing New Age Movement, is another.

The search for spiritual experience always involves questions of good and evil. It seems no society has ever existed without categories of ethical rightness or wrongness; and the roots of these are usually understood to be located in the realms of the spirit, as expressed in myth and religion.[1] The current situation in our own culture is no exception. An interesting example of this can be seen in the attempts of proponents of New Age spirituality to deal with questions of evil. One of the hallmarks of the movement has been its eclecticism, affirming numerous diverse religious approaches as equally valid (conspicuously excluding orthodox Christianity): varieties of Buddhism and Hinduism, North American native traditional religion, shamanistic practices from other cultures, 'benign' witchcraft, various spiritually oriented psychotherapies, occultism and mediumship, now called channelling.

Channelling illustrates the problem of such spiritual naïveté very well. Within the last decade, numerous people claiming to be channels for spiritual 'energies' or entities have come forward as bearers of enlightenment. The response of devotees of New Age spirituality has generally been that of belief and adulation, including very often the paying of exorbitant fees. The monistic orientation of much New Age thinking, which often incorporates both good and evil into 'god' or the absolute, creates great difficulties in dealing with evil in concrete terms. Yet New Agers, being human like everyone else, eventually do not like to be conned.

One rather poignant example of this is found in a recent book by Joe Fisher.[2] The author, a convinced New Ager and believer in the legitimacy of channelling, made numerous contacts over a period of time with what he believed to be benign spirits. Hungry for corroborative evidence of the information he was being given by these 'guides', he embarked on an intensive investigation which took him literally around the world. Much to his chagrin, he found that the entities were lying. He concluded that there are such things as malevolent spirits which seek to harm or at least mislead. Fisher, though disillusioned, did not move into complete scepticism, nor did he leave the spiritual path he had chosen. Rather, he tried to address spiritual evil and deception while remaining within a (somewhat chastened) New Age framework.

The reality of spiritual evil has always been (at least theoretically) recognized within historic Christianity. The existence of devils has never been seriously questioned among those calling themselves Christians until relatively recent times. Evangelical Christians have generally stayed in line with classical Christian belief. However, the last few years have seen a tremendous surge of interest in the existence and activity of the devil, and in the spiritual warfare in which Christians are engaged. When this writer first conceived of writing a thesis on spiritual warfare, such was not the case. It seemed then that the conception of the Christian as a soldier in enemy territory (so prominent in the English Puritans) was lacking in our time, and needed recovering. As the content of these pages was being researched, a great deal of material began to appear from Christian publishing houses, addressing questions of spiritual warfare from various angles. Much of this was, perhaps, due to a reawakening in the Christian public, seeing the growth of spiritual and occultic practices on every side. Thus this study, focussing on the English Puritans and their view of spiritual warfare, at its completion exists in a somewhat different environment than at its inception. Once the author conceived of it as exploring a valuable and missing perspective. Now, it presents an older view of a topic that has become of great interest again.

This book, then, asks the question, what is the Puritan view of spiritual warfare? The Puritans do not exist in a vacuum. They are inheritors of sixteen centuries of Christian history (and as they use the Hebrew Scriptures much more extensively than many Christians do now, one can push their pedigree back another millennium as well).

Although they are the immediate heirs of the Reformation and the legacy of Luther and Calvin, one can say that Puritan demonology is a catholic demonology. Despite their well-known opposition to the papacy as it existed in their own time, their roots are deep into the general tradition of Christian orthodoxy, stretching back through such figures as Bernard of Clairvaux (whom they often quote), to the Church Fathers and thence (and I would argue most significantly) into the Bible.

Like the great majority of people living in their time (and apparently in our time as well), the Puritans believe in occult phenomena. Some write books giving detailed accounts of apparently supernatural occurrences. William Perkins' *A Discourse of the Damned Art of Witchcraft* was published in 1610.[3] The prolific Richard Baxter is not wanting here; one of his works is entitled *The Certainty of the Worlds of Spirits,* published about eighty years later.[4] Much of the content of the book is indicated by its subtitle: *Fully evinced by unquestionable histories of apparitions and witchcrafts, operations, voices, etc.* The American Puritan, Cotton Mather, wrote *The Wonders of the Invisible World* during the witch trials in New England, covering similar ground to that of Perkins and Baxter.[5]

Certainly some of the content of these books reflects credulity. This may not, however, tell the whole story. The visceral reaction and revulsion of rationalist historians and anthropologists to the witch craze is understandable; but they may be guilty of some credulity themselves. The resurgence of modern Satanism, wherein various individuals and groups have been discovered to be devoted to evil as evil, demonstrates that such devotion is possible;

and if possible now, certainly it was possible in other times and places as well.[6]

The Puritan view of spiritual warfare, however, while it includes the belief that satanic witchcraft exists, does not find its focus there. In fact, taken in the context of the whole of Puritan teaching, witchcraft is not a major theme. This book seeks to present an accurate picture of the mainstream Puritan outlook, centring on the image captured in the title: *The Embattled Christian*. John Bunyan gives literary expression to this image in his portrayal of the pilgrim-warrior in *The Pilgrim's Progress*. In this he simply expresses what is found everywhere in Puritan writing, sometimes appearing scattered throughout various expositions, sometimes in specific sermons or extended works.

The Puritan interest in this subject is very much a pastoral interest. In a sense, they are not interested at all in the devil. They are not indulging in occult speculation for its own sake, to satisfy their curiosity. One might say their demonology is a subset of their doctrine of sanctification, or of their ecclesiology. That is, their pastoral concern is to help the church (made up of individual Christians), or Christians (who together make up the church) to live a holy life to the Lord. Their primary source for pastoral instruction is the Scriptures. The Bible, as well as their own experience, tells them that Christians as individuals, and Christians as the church, are impeded, tempted, deceived, discouraged by a powerful spiritual antagonist. The interest of this book, then, is to investigate how the Puritans describe this enemy; how they depict Christians caught in the struggle against such a foe; and how they seek to equip Christians and the church in order to do battle successfully.

5

The work thus falls into three major divisions, which attempt to answer the following questions: first, who is the enemy? This section (Chapter 2) explores the Puritan exposition of Ephesians 6:11–12, Paul's well-known description of 'principalities, . . . powers, . . . the rulers of the darkness of this world, . . . spiritual wickedness in high places.' Second, why and how are the saints vulnerable? Chapter 3 views the Puritan picture of the saints in this world, especially in regard to the weaknesses that make Christians targets of satanic attack. Third, since the people of God stand in great danger, with what are they to defend themselves? Chapter 4 thus investigates the resources available to Christians—the armour described in Ephesians 6:13–18—which they are to use to engage in spiritual warfare, or as William Gurnall puts it:

A Magazine opened, from whence the Christian is furnished with Spiritual Arms for the Battle, helped on with his Armour, and taught the use of his Weapon.[7]

METHODOLOGY

Regarding methodology, several comments are in order.

The focus of these pages is deliberately, as well as necessarily, narrow: I attempt to condense from a mass of literature (Puritan prolixity is well known) the explicitly Puritan view of the questions outlined above. Thus comparatively little is said about the historical development of the doctrines considered. The book studies one historical example; it is not a chronological study. Nor does it attempt to view the Puritan outlook by placing it over against another school of thought, such as the teaching of the Roman Catholic Church at that time. Such contrasts appear occasionally and serve to illustrate and define the Puritan view. However, they are not my subject. I intend rather to pinpoint the Puritan perspective, in itself, as accurately as possible.

Another point to be made is that this is not an essay on the Puritans' involvement in the politics of their day. The Puritan era was filled with social and political ferment and conflict, and the threat of war (as well as actual war) had an enormous impact on those living in such circumstances. The warfare theme of this book certainly could be viewed through a socio-political lens; but again, it would be a different book, and so such questions are not primarily addressed.[8]

The references most used are primary sources, the reason for which is explained in much the same manner as the question of focus. It seems to the author that in delineating a Puritan view of spiritual warfare, the persons most to be consulted are the Puritans themselves. The body of their extant work is vast and quite easily accessible; the majority of the relevant works are in English, and many have been reprinted in this century. Also, the question here addressed is very specific; they speak to it with great force, clarity, and a largely undivided voice, as the body of the work will show. Secondary works are referred to at times, to illustrate or buttress the argument, or to help in describing the context of the Puritan era.

In this book, the doorway to the Puritan literature on spiritual combat is William Gurnall's *The Christian in Complete Armour*. It is a later Puritan work, originally published in the 1650s and 1660s. Gurnall's work stands at the heart of my interest, and is the primary source consulted. Reference is made throughout to various other

major Puritan writers, who serve to demonstrate agreement, sometimes difference of nuance, and occasionally
disagreement. Some of the earlier Puritan references to be
considered are William Perkins' works *A Discourse of the
Damned Art of Witchcraft* and *The Combat Between
Christ and the Divell Displayed*, and Paul Bayne's *Exposition of Ephesians*. Another Puritan writer addressing this
theme in the early seventeenth century is John Downame,
whose *The Christian Warfare* was published in 1608. By
1634, this work had gone through four editions.[9] William
Gouge's *The Whole Armour of God* is another Puritan
work from the early 1600s. The edition consulted by this
writer says it was revised by the author in 1627, 'and now
the fourth time published and inlarged'.[10] Reference is also
made to Richard Sibbes, renowned Puritan from the same
era.

The works of Puritans writing more in the middle to
later seventeenth century are also consulted, such men as
William Bridge, John Owen, Thomas Brooks, Thomas
Manton, Thomas Watson, and Richard Baxter. These of
course include that most renowned of all Puritan works,
Bunyan's *The Pilgrim's Progress*. A younger contemporary of William Gurnall, Richard Gilpin, in 1677 published
a work devoted completely to the subject of spiritual warfare against the devil: *Daemonologia Sacra; or, a Treatise
of Satan's Temptations*. About five hundred pages in
length, Gilpin's work is very similar in content to
Gurnall's. Matthew Poole's *Commentary on Ephesians*
and Matthew Henry's *Commentary* are consulted as well.

A few things should be noted regarding purely technical
matters:

First, the version of the Bible which I have quoted

throughout is, ironically as well as logically enough, the King James Version.

Second, since Gurnall is referred to the most extensively, he will generally not be quoted by use of numbered notes as the other sources are. Rather, references to his work will be marked throughout the text in parentheses.

Third, quotes from several of the older works will basically be reproduced as they stand in the manuscripts. Many of these have not become available in new editions, thus the spelling is not always uniform nor according to current standards. The only correction undertaken by the author is to standardize the letters 'u' and 'v' for clarity.

Fourth, it may be noticed that the entire book is written as much as possible in the present tense. The reason for this is the writer's perspective toward these older texts as living voices. While it is true that this is an investigation in historical theology/spirituality, and thus a largely descriptive exercise, it is nevertheless the author's opinion that such work is best done as dialogue. Any valid attempt to understand a text means allowing it to speak to one as a living voice, not viewing it as an inanimate 'object of interest' to be investigated and remarked upon as a dead relic. Also, it is this writer's opinion that the questions addressed in this thesis are very much live issues today, and that the Puritan contribution is a needed and valuable word across time.

BIOGRAPHICAL SKETCH OF WILLIAM GURNALL
As William Gurnall's book is the central work considered in these pages, a brief biography is in order.

The Christian in Complete Armour was widely known and used both during and after its author's lifetime. It remains so today; the Banner of Truth Trust has published reprints in 1964, 1974, 1979, 1983, and 1990. Not a great deal is known, however, about the author himself, possible reasons for which will be considered shortly.

Biographical resources on Gurnall are limited. A Roman Catholic antiquarian named Hugh McKeon—an admirer of Gurnall—published two small works in the early nineteenth century. The first, published in 1829, has an extended title beginning with *An inquiry into the rights of the poor of the Parish of Lavenham, in Suffolk.* This is followed by various comments and the announcement of several biographical sketches, including Rev. William Gurnall, formerly Rector of Lavenham, and the author of *The Christian in Compleat Armour,* etc.

McKeon's second work was published in 1830, with an equally extended title. In this case Gurnall is the main topic: *An inquiry into the birth-place, parentage, life, and writings, of the Reverend William Gurnall, M.A. Formerly rector of Lavenham, in Suffolk, and author of 'The Christian in Compleat Armour, etc.'* Appended to this section of the title is the famous quote from John Newton, 'Were I confined to one book, besides my Bible, I dare say Gurnall's *Christian Armour* would be my choice.'

Another biographical source is found in the edition of Gurnall's book published by Blackie and Son, Glasgow, in 1864. J. C. Ryle contributed 'A biographical account of the author' to this edition, reproduced in Banner of Truth's reprint. Ryle's sketch, while containing a good deal of his own research, relied heavily on the second work of McKeon.

William Gurnall's mother was Catherine Dressit; his father was Gregory Gurnall. They married on December 31, 1615, at St. Margaret's Church, Lynn, Norfolk.

William, their first child, was born late the following year, and baptized on November 17, 1616. He attended grammar school in Lynn; not much else is known of his childhood.[11] Gregory Gurnall was something of a public man in Lynn; he was an alderman at the time of William's birth, and in 1624 became mayor of the borough. He died on October 14, 1631 while William was still a youth.[12]

The foundation for Gurnall's Puritanism may have been laid during his youth in Lynn. Norfolk County was known as a Puritan enclave. The Puritan preachers Samuel Fairclough and John Arrowsmith ministered in Lynn;[13] years later, 'John Arrowsmith of Lynne' is listed amongst the members of the Assembly at Westminster.[14] The young Gurnall may have been catechized, or at any rate influenced, by such men.

At the age of fifteen, William Gurnall received a Lynn scholarship to Emmanuel College, Cambridge. He entered the college in 1632, taking the B.A. degree in 1635, and the M.A. in 1639.[15] Emmanuel was a Puritan college practically from its founding in 1585. Numerous leading Puritans of the seventeenth century were educated there, including John Preston, William Bridge, Stephen Charnock, Thomas Watson, and Matthew Poole, to name only a few of the multitude.[16] William Gurnall may have acquired his Puritan convictions at Emmanuel; or his experience there may have simply confirmed the faith of his childhood.

In the years immediately following Gurnall's departure from Cambridge, England exploded into Civil War, the Puritan-dominated Parliament facing off against King Charles I. Sir Simonds D'Ewes, one of the parliamentarians who would have preferred to resolve the conflict without arms,[17] was 'patron of the living of Lavenham, and chief proprietor in the parish.'[18] In 1644 he offered William Gurnall the rectory of Lavenham,[19] apparently at the request of the parishioners. Hugh McKeon infers from this that Gurnall, already resident in Lavenham and perhaps officiating as curate, 'became so popular with the people as to be deemed an acquisition to the parish.'[20]

The new rector was a single man, but not for long. The following year he married Sarah Mott, the only daughter of another minister, Rev. Thomas Mott. During their marriage they had ten children, perhaps more.[21] In this Gurnall seems to have been a true Puritan also, as the Puritans were robust lovers, and strong believers in the sanctity of sexuality, and marriage and family life.[22]

William and Sarah Gurnall remained in Lavenham for the rest of their life together, William continuing his work there as rector until his death in 1679. It seems that during much of his ministry, Gurnall was not a healthy man.[23]

Perhaps one of the most significant events for understanding Gurnall's unique life is the Act of Uniformity of 1662. Under this act, two thousand nonconforming ministers were forced out of the Church of England. Gurnall, in contrast to his Puritan brethren, signed the required declaration, and received Episcopal ordination and institution at Lavenham that August. Gurnall as a conforming Puritan was in a decidedly peculiar position, since nearly every named Puritan at the time was ejected, including Thomas Mott, Gurnall's own father-in-law. Ryle points out that conformity, while allowing Gurnall to retain his position as rector, severely tarnished his reputation.[24] In 1665 Gurnall was attacked in print. The author accused Gurnall of 'horrible defilements', and of being a member of an 'anti-Christian priesthood and brethren in the same iniquity with himself.' The title reads as follows:

Covenant Renouncers Desperate Apostates, opened in two letters, written by a Christian friend to Mr. W. Gurnall, of Lavenham in Suffolk, which may indefinitely serve as an admonition to all such Presbyterian ministers or others, who have forced their conscience, not only to leap over, but to renounce their solemn covenant obligation to endeavour a reformation according to God's word, and the extirpation of all prelatical superstitions, and contrary thereunto conform to those superstitious vanities against which they had so solemnly sworn. Printed in Antiturncoat Street, and sold at the sign of Truth's Delight, right opposite to Backsliding Alley. 4to, 1665.[25]

It is the contention of Ryle that Gurnall's conformity is the reason for the absence of biographical literature. Baxter, Manton, Owen, Goodwin and so many others seceded from the established church; Gurnall remained within it.[26]

Obviously, many folk live without attracting much notice from the world at large; lack of detailed biography in such cases is not a 'mystery'. Most human beings live and die in relative anonymity. The lack of detailed biographical reference to Gurnall may be 'just one of those things'. Yet the Puritan epoch is renowned for its attention to biography, and for most prominent Puritans a generous amount of information is available. Thus it is odd for a Puritan writer to produce a mammoth work like *The Christian in Complete Armour* and yet remain personally obscure. Ryle's analysis may be correct.

Within Gurnall's book there are indicators of his outlook, which may help explain why he decided to stay within the Church of England. In one passage, where he is describing the devil's use of deceit to waylay the Christian, Gurnall says:

By bewailing the corruption of the church in its administrations, he draws unstable souls from it, and amuseth them, till at last they fall into a giddiness, and can see no church at all in being. (I:75)

Gurnall resists the spirit of anarchy, in which people angry at ecclesiastical abuses leap, as it were, from the frying pan into the fire. Written prior to the Act of Uniformity, Gurnall's comments show the direction of his thinking as he speaks of those he calls 'sect-makers':

These are they who pretend more to purity of worship than others, and profess they separate on account of their conscience, because they cannot suffer themselves so much as touch them that are unclean by joining with them in holy ordinances. (I:471, 472)

Gurnall goes on to say that not all those who have separated from communion are pretenders; yet his distress is apparent over professing Christians who, in the name of purity of worship, separate from the church, only to slide into denial of the Gospel, and every degradation. It seems clear that he speaks as a sorrowing pastor, seeing the moral and spiritual consequences in the lives of people who cut themselves away from the Christian community. This pastoral concern, and deep misgiving about separation and fragmentation of the church, may help explain Gurnall's willingness to stay within the Church of England when so many others went out.

Despite the fact that the personal biography of Gurnall is limited, his magnificent book remains as a monumental testimony to the concerns of the man. Gurnall's teaching, and that of all the Puritans, is intended to prepare the saints for battle. The next chapter presents the Puritan view of those against whom the saints fight.

2

The Enemy: Identity and Character

Puritan 'thoroughness' in engaging with matters of the Christian life is well known. This holds true as they confront the Christian's spiritual enemy. They do not simply describe the enemy, and leave it at that. The description is always given with a pastoral and practical end in view: here is the enemy, according to the Word of God; here is what God expects you to do about him (or them). William Gurnall typifies this approach both in the detail with which he treats the enemy, and the thoroughness with which he applies his teaching to his hearers' lives. Gurnall's description of the identity and character of the enemy is an exposition of Ephesians 6:12:

For we wrestle not against flesh and blood, but against principalities, against powers, against the rulers of the darkness of this world, against spiritual wickedness in high places.

Gurnall follows the order given by the apostle. He notes that some writers are of the opinion that Paul is describing a sort of hierarchy of evil, with a monarch, and distinct orders and ranks arrayed beneath him. Such is the view, for instance, of Paul Bayne, successor to William Perkins at Christ's College, Cambridge.[1] Gurnall agrees that there is such a diabolical hierarchy, citing Matthew 9:34 where Jesus is accused of being in league with the 'prince' of devils. However, Gurnall does not interpret the categories of Ephesians 6:12 as hierarchical (or as he says, 'distributive'). Rather, he takes these as descriptive collectively of all the devils, for this reason:

Some of these branches cannot be meant of distinct orders, but promiscuously of all as spiritual wickedness; it being not proper to one to be spirits or wicked, but common to all. (I:130)

The idea that the descriptions of Ephesians 6:12 are meant to be taken of the devils generally seems to be the more common Puritan position. William Gouge, whose *The Whole Armour of God* was published when Gurnall was a boy, propounds this view:

From these severall branches many collect divers and distinct orders of Devils . . . For my part, I thinke these distinctions in this place over-curious . . . I rather take these titles to be used by the Apostle, to set forth their conditions and effects.[2]

PRINCIPALITIES
Gurnall begins with 'principalities'. He defines this term as pointing to the devils'[3] government in the world (I:130). William Perkins long before spoke of Satan's attempts

in the state of his apostasie . . . that he might set up in the world, a spirituall regiment of sinne, as a meane to encounter the kingdom of grace, and if it were possible, to bring the same to ruine.[4]

The Puritans recognize the existence of a diabolical kingdom. Satan is a great prince, says Gurnall, quoting

Jesus, who calls the devil the 'prince of this world' (John 14:30). His rule, however, differs from that of earthly kings, who rule the bodies and purses of their subjects for a limited time—and are often pulled down by them as well (England's recent Civil Wars, culminating in the beheading of Charles I in 1649,[5] would have given Gurnall's hearers drastic illustration of his point). The devil rules the hearts of his subjects. Referring to Revelation 13:4, in which the world is shown worshipping both the beast and the dragon who empowers him, Gurnall says this is a true description of the wicked in relation to the devil. The wicked worship the devil; and in fact he will settle for nothing less than religious obeisance (I:131).

Religious homage to the devil is rendered whether wittingly or unwittingly; whether willingly or no. For the Puritans, religion outside Christ presents no other alternative. Religious service is given to the devil even if a person is not religious; and religious people who seek to worship God outside or against the Christian revelation are in fact worshipping the devil.[6]

The totality of the devil's rule finds an echo, for Gurnall, in the Turkish absolute monarchs: 'where their laws are written in no other tables than in the proud sultan's breast' (I:131). A modern illustration of this can be found in what one writer reported regarding a supposed remark of the president of Iraq: 'A law is a piece of paper on which we write one or two lines, then sign "Saddam Hussein".'[7]

William Gouge concurs with Gurnall's exposition, noting that the term 'principalities' (or 'governments') applies because the devils have 'great rule, power, and dominion, not so much over other Devils, as over wicked men.'[8]

There is grim irony in this rulership of the devil over sinful humanity. The hallmark of human sin is rebellion against the rule of God; the desire—and the conceit—of being a law unto oneself. Rather than bringing the autonomy men and women desire, it brings them under the arbitrary rule of the devil; rather than finding freedom, they are exposed to diabolical compulsion.

Thus Satan gives law to the poor sinner, who is bound and must obey, though the law be writ with his own blood, and the creature hath nothing but damnation for fulfilling the devil's lust. (I:131)[9]

Gurnall finds this satanic law expressed in Romans 8:2 as the 'law of sin and death' (I:131). This seems exegetically questionable; at least Satan's rule is not the prime focus here. Rather, as the context indicates (so also in Romans 7:21 and 23) this 'law of sin' is what Paul also calls the 'flesh' in Romans 7:18. John Owen defines this law in his work on indwelling sin:

The flesh, which is the seat and throne of this law, yea, which indeed is this law, is in some sense the man himself, . . . it is an indwelling law inclining and moving to sin, as an inward habit or principle, . . .[10]

Nevertheless, Gurnall's point is valid: the devil's rule over human beings is effective because of the law of sin already present within them, which is responsive to Satan's overtures.

This subjection to the devil is not recognized as such by many who are under his dominion. The devil, however, does have human favourites. Human rulers have their ministers of state 'whom they employ for the safety and enlargement of their territories'; the devil likewise employs human ministers for propagating his own wicked purposes (I:131). Gurnall uses the example of Elymas, the sorcerer encountered by the Apostle Paul on Cyprus, as such a one (Acts 13:6–11). The Puritans teach that some human beings, on familiar terms with the devil, more or less openly express his rule on earth. Some are more the children of the devil than others. Christ had his beloved disciple; and Satan those that lie in his very bosom, and know what is in his heart (I:132).

The matter of witchcraft is very near the surface in this statement; Gurnall's use of the example of Elymas the sorcerer is perhaps indicative of this. The Puritans do not say that the only conscious servants of the devil are witches; far from it.[11] For them, however, as for most people of their time and place, witches are the clearest and most fearsome illustration of such servitude.[12] Jeffrey Burton Russell designates the period from approximately A.D. 1400 to 1700 as a time in which witchcraft came to be understood as explicit, conscious service to the devil as the devil. Central to this understanding is the idea of a pact made between the witch and the devil.[13] The Puritans generally agree with this conception.

While the Puritans teach that some human beings consciously dedicate themselves to evil, even these are not really the devil's compatriots. They are simply his prime instruments, those most immediately useful to him, after which they too are discarded:

Indeed he doth not so much share with the sinner in all, but is owner of all he hath; so that the devil is the merchant, and the sinner but the broker to trade for him, who at last puts all his gains into the devil's purse. (I:132)

William Gurnall discusses Satan's attainment of rulership from three perspectives: Satan's conquest, human election or choice, and God's permission. First, through the exercise of his power and cunning, the devil succeeded in conquering humanity, and bringing the race under his dominion. Gurnall points out, however, that the exercise of superior power does not give legitimacy to rule: 'But conquest is a cracked title. . . . a thief on the throne is no better than a private one on the road, . . . Neither doth that prove good with process of time which was evil at first' (I:132).

Other Puritans make the same point: William Gouge remarks that the devil's rule is unlawful, his government that of a tyrannous invader.[14] Might does not make right. Satan's claim of conquest is that of a usurper, like Hitler with his excuses for attacking his neighbouring countries in Europe. So the devil's power over human beings is an illegitimate usurpation of the power which belongs only to God, and he maintains it only by the method always necessary to criminal aggressors: coercion, the rule of power and fear over his subjects.[15]

Second, humanity has placed itself—individually and corporately—under the rule of Satan voluntarily; this Gurnall refers to as election (I:132). Gouge says: 'For the Devil's vassals (which are all the wicked of the world) they slavishly and willingly yeeld themselves to his government and tyranny'.[16]

Gurnall agrees. The fact of human election of Satan as ruler, however, has not changed the fact of God's continued sovereignty. Humanity's relationship to God is damaged, but by creation men and women remain God's creatures, and cannot escape God's right of rule (I:132).

Third, the evil one may claim his rulership as a gift of God himself, as he did when tempting Christ (Luke 4:5, 6). Gurnall points out that this is a half-truth, used to gain 'credit to some lie at the end of it' (I:132). It is true, says Gurnall, that God has delivered the world over to Satan— but not as his possession to use as he will. Rather, Satan is prince of the world, not by God's grace, but by God's permission (I:132). The question is, why? For what purpose would God permit such a usurper and destroyer access to his own creation? Gurnall brings forward three answers, very common themes running through Puritan literature.

First, the devil's rule is an act of judgment, a pouring out of God's wrath because of humanity's revolt. God's sovereignty even over evil is a very marked emphasis of Puritanism:

The devil is God's slave, man the devil's. Sin hath set the devil on the creature's back; and now he hurries him without mercy, as he did the swine, till he be choked with flames, if mercy interpose not. (I:133)[17]

Gurnall's contemporary Richard Gilpin, writing a few years after Gurnall's book was published, makes the same point. God makes use of the devil's power 'as an executioner of wrath against his enemies.'[18] The Puritans sound this note repeatedly.

Second, God uses Satan to test and build his own people. Puritan confidence of victory over the devil has much to do with their conviction of God's absolute sovereignty, including those affairs in their own lives where they experience satanic attack. Thomas Manton, another Puritan whose age and time of ministry correspond very closely to Gurnall's, has this to say:

This cruel spirit is held in the chains of an irresistible providence,. . .which is a great satisfaction to the faithful: all things which concern our trial are determined and ordered by God. If we be free, let us bless God for it,. . .if tempted, when we are in Satan's hands, remember Satan is in God's hand.[19]

The devil is thus not only God's slave; he and his whole council are a pack of fools to God. Gurnall goes so far as to say that as great men use wild beasts for sport, so God uses Satan and his servants, 'to manifest his wisdom in the taking of them' (I:102). Thus the devils, with all their scheming, end up serving ends opposite to what they intend; these auspicious 'principalities' serve as tools for the building up of God's people. As William Perkins writes, God uses Satan, 'To waken and rouze up the godly . . . to trie and proove his people, whether they will cleave to him and his word.'[20]

In attacking the saints, the devil's principality is ineffectual; he is 'but a bungler that hurts and hacks his own legs with his own axe' (I:102). Gurnall uses an arresting image to describe this: 'Thus God sets the devil to catch the devil, and lays, as it were, his own counsels under Satan's wings, and makes him hatch them' (I:102).

Third, God also permits this principality because of the glory which will be brought about through redemption. Gurnall says redemption, even above creation and preservation of the universe, will bring glory to God. Achieving redemption against devilish resistance 'adds to the nuptial song the triumph of a conqueror, who hath rescued his bride out of the hands of Satan, as he was leading her to the chambers of hell' (I:133).

The Puritans thus teach that God, by allowing such a principality of evil, brings about a greater good. He does not trivialize or assimilate or justify the evil; rather, he overcomes the evil as evil, and in so doing brings about his own greater purpose.

POWERS

The devils' position as principalities is meaningless without the power to enforce and maintain their rule. The Puritans, while uniformly insistent on the devils' creatureliness (thus rejecting any dualism of equality), nevertheless make much of their power. William Perkins early on exemplifies this when he speaks of 'The Power of this Prince of darknesse, beeing above the might of all sensible Creatures, and every way seconded by the greatnesse of his knowledge and experience'.[21]

William Gurnall refers to many of the biblical images which are descriptive of the devil's power. Luke 11:21 describes him as the strong man; so strong, says Gurnall, that he keeps his house in peace in defiance of all of Adam's sons, none of whom can cope with his might. Only Christ is able to destroy him (I:140). He is also called the roaring lion 'which beast commands the whole forest. If he roars, all tremble' (I:140).

In Revelation 12:9 the devil is called the great dragon, who with his tail (which Gurnall interprets as the devil's wicked human servants) wreaks great destruction (I:140). The image of the dragon occurs often in Puritan literature. John Downame in his *Christian Warfare* refers particularly to the dragon's antiquity as enhancing his power:

Yea, an old serpent, which being the subtilest of beasts, hath his craft redoubled by his age and experience, . . .[22]

Satan is also called the god of this world (2 Corinthians 4:4).

This godlikeness entails the exercise of vast power, as Downame again notes: in respect to his own power in the world, particularly in regard to the inability of humans to resist him,

he is after a sort omnipotent, that is, able to doe what he list, if he were not restrained by God's divine power.[23]

Gurnall observes that this status as a god is conferred or confirmed by sinful human beings themselves, who worship and fear Satan as the saints do God (I:140).[24]

While the various names given the devil in Scripture are indicators of his power, his created nature as an angelic being contains actual power as one of its characteristics. Gurnall quotes Psalm 103:20, 'Bless the Lord, ye his angels, that excel in strength' (I:140). In the hierarchy of creation, Gurnall places angels at the top, humanity a little lower than the angels, followed by the beasts, then plant life. The spirituality of the angelic nature is where Gurnall locates their superior power (I:140). This conviction that untrammelled power inheres in the spiritual nature is common to all the Puritans. William Perkins, for example, writes that the devil

is a spirit of wonderfull power and might, able to . . . confound the creatures inferiour to him in nature and condition . . .[25]

Perkins, in fact, feels that the devil's power is significantly increased by his fall. Created as a perfect being, Satan's power before his fall was awesome. Since that time it has actually grown, energized by the malice he bears toward humanity, and 'specially the seede of the woman', the incarnate Son of God.[26]

William Gouge, by contrast, says that the fall actually lessened the power of the fallen angels:

For whensoever there was any opposition betwixt good and evill Angels, the evil were alwaies foiled . . . But in regard to human beings, the power of the evil angels is still so vast as to be virtually undiminished: 'still they remain to be as powerfull to doe mischiefe, as they were to doe good.'[27]

Gurnall's emphasis is a little different:

The devil lost, indeed, by his fall, much of his power in relation to that holy and happy estate in which he was created, but not his natural abilities; he is an angel still, and hath an angel's power. (I:141)

Human beings, in contrast, are weighed down with a 'lump of flesh' (I:140). Richard Gilpin remarks in a similarly negative way about

the clog and hindrance of corporeity. . . . flesh and blood are a disadvantage and hindrance to the activity of a spirit.[28]

Such statements sound rather like semi-gnostic attacks on the goodness of the body, the superior spirit trapped and encumbered in the inferior flesh. Gurnall, again, says the soul 'is forced to row with a strength suitable to its weak partner' (I:140). Gurnall, at least, clarifies what he is saying a few pages later; he seems to be referring to the disability humans have received bodily as a result of the fall. The frailty of human bodily experience is a result of degeneration; the human soul is 'sunk beneath its primitive extraction; . . . the body, which was a lightsome house, is now become a prison to it; that which was its servant, is now become its master' (I:143).

Angels, even fallen angels, have no such hindrance; even

the devils retain the power inherent in their original created nature. Gurnall paints an intimidating picture of these discarnate beings, all swiftness, clarity, intellectual acuity:

The devils being angels have no such encumbrance, no fumes from a fleshly part to cloud their understanding, which is clear and piercing; no clog at their heel to retard their motion, . . . (I:140)

Material force is useless against such beings. Gurnall illustrates this contention from the Hebrew Scriptures, with the story of the angel's appearance to Samson's father, Manoah (Judges 13:20). The angel departs by rising amidst the flames of the sacrifice (I:141). This theme—the ineffectiveness of human resistance to demonic power—gives occasion in Gurnall's exposition for one of his rare criticisms of the seventeenth-century Roman Catholic Church. He notes the superstition of those in his day who think the devil is frightened off by various ritual actions, or objects such as relics, crucifixes, or holy water (I:141). Keith Thomas refers to these as 'the magic of the medieval church.'[29] This criticism sounds a major Puritan (and Reformation) emphasis, the uselessness of any mechanical or magical technique in religious things.

Gurnall contends that Roman Catholic 'magic' is worse than useless, and that the devil cares nothing for such things. But he does not stop with this critique of the papacy. God's own ordinances, when made into a magic spell by placing fleshly confidence in them, are also ineffective against the devil. Gurnall thus repudiates any method, Catholic or Protestant, that seeks to control the devil through some incantation or talisman. He refers believers, instead, directly to God:

It must be a stronger than the strong man [that] must bind him, and none [is] stronger but God, the Father of spirits. (I:141)

The number of the devils also adds to their power. John Downame speaks of them as being virtually numberless.[30]

The Christian is not facing a solitary enemy. Rather, the devils are a great multitude, enough to 'beleaguer the whole earth' (I:141). Gurnall estimates the number of these entities to be very high indeed; they are Satan's troops 'haunting and watching' every human born (I:141). He supports his opinion from Mark's Gospel, chapter 5, which recounts the story of the Gadarene demoniac, inhabited by a 'legion' of spirits (verse 9). If, for a special purpose, the devil can spare this many to attend one person, how many might there be in his entire retinue?[31]

Gurnall compares Satan and his angels, cast from heaven, to a disbanded army (of which the English had plenty of experience on their own soil, due to the Civil Wars). After a war the countryside is full of debauched soldiers, making for dangerous travel: 'we hear then of murderers and robberies from all quarters' (I:141). Ever since the rebels were thrown from heaven, 'they have straggled here below, endeavouring to do mischief to the children of men, especially travelling in heaven's road' (I:141).

Thus the Christian is likely to find it a difficult road to heaven, as one must march straight through such a multitude in order to reach one's destination (I:141).

The Puritans also teach that the power of the devils is formidable due to their order and unity. Downame remarks that the spiritual enemies of humanity are in total agreement regarding their intentions:

For though they be an huge multitude, yet they combine themselves together, as if they were but one, in seeking our destruction.[32]

Devils are no fools regarding the nature of their divine enemy. They have been on intimate acquaintance with God, and know the vastness of his power. Therefore they know their kingdom is finished unless they are united; there is no mutiny amongst them.[33] Gurnall quotes the testimony of Jesus in this regard, where the Lord observes that Satan does not fight against himself (Matthew 12:26). At the same time, unity of purpose does not mean that the devils bear any love to one another:

That heavenly fire cannot live in a devil's bosom; yet there is unity and order as to this—they are all agreed in their design against God and man. Hatred, not love, unites them. (I:141)

Gurnall describes a diabolical conformity that is quite unprecedented even amongst the wicked of the human race. Totalitarian movements always seek complete uniformity, not only of external obedience but of inward thought as well; none are ever completely successful. Gurnall maintains that in hell there is such accord. He also believes that these spirits endeavour to bring their human instruments to a similar state of unity—unity not necessarily with their human companions, but with the devils. Thus the cursed spirits are 'not contented with their bare obedience, but where they can obtain it do require an express oath of their servants to be true to them, as in witches' (I:142). (Note again the idea of pact, the devil's bargain, as the ultimate in human degradation: specific, conscious devotion to evil as evil.)

The devils' power is also illustrated by their mighty

works: in the elements, in the 'sensible' world, and primarily in the world of the human mind (I:142). Gurnall and all the Puritans believe strongly that Satan can move and influence the material world. This has already been noted in the Introduction, where several Puritan writings on occult phenomena are listed.[34] The devil can do no truly creative work, according to the Puritans; he can only work with and within the existing creation. Gouge says of the devil:

He himselfe is a creature, his power is a created power: and therefore limited within the bounds of a creature . . . Hee is not able to doe anything simply above, or directly against, that course which the Lord hath ordained unto his creatures . . .[35]

Though the Puritans oppose the idea that Satan can work miracles (that ability belonging only to God), they do teach that various signs and wonders are performed by him. Their conception of the 'natural world' is not so narrow as the modern 'closed box', naturalistic conception. The invisible world of spirits is still part of the created order, and thus the parameters bounding what is possible include action and interchange between the visible and invisible sectors of creation. This is why William Perkins can say that the devil's action is shown

for the most part, by workes of wonder, transcendent in regard of ordinarie capacitie, and diversely dispensed by his chosen instruments of both sexes, sometime in matter of Divination, sometime by Inchantment, sometime by rare sleigts and delusions; otherwhiles by hurting, by curing, by raising of Tempests, by speedie convayance and transportation from place to place . . .[36]

Referring to the devil's activities as described in the

book of Job, Gurnall reiterates that Satan cannot truly create. However, he can, if let loose, 'go to God's storehouse, and make use of these in such a sort as no man can stand before him' (I:142). Gurnall believes Satan is operative in certain extraordinarily violent storms, such as those that destroyed Job's children. He reasons that if human inventiveness can produce marvels such as gunpowder, the devil is even more capable of drawing forth nature's power—always, of course, with his own destructive ends in mind regarding humanity.[37]

Along with demonic power over the the elements, the Puritans assert the power of the devils to influence the 'sensitive' world, the world of living creatures, including the human body. Gurnall notes the demon-driven swine in Mark 5:11–13. He refers to the diseases experienced by Job as the 'print of Satan's fangs on his flesh' (I:142), doing suddenly that which normal illness would take longer to produce. Gouge says of the power of the devil over both human beings and animals: 'He can cast them into the fire and water, grievously vexe and torment them, and inflict sore diseases upon them'.[38] Thus Gurnall and the other Puritans definitely believe that some illness, at least, can be seen as the direct action of the devil.

Yet in comparison with the devil's real focus of attack, the Puritans consider his action in the inanimate and 'sensitive' world 'small game' (I:142). Despite their insistence on the devil's ability to work lying signs and wonders, and their descriptions of occult phenomena, the Puritans do not see these as central to the devil's work. Here another strong, and characteristically Puritan, emphasis appears:

His great spite is at the souls of men, which I shall call the intellectual world; his cruelty to the body is for the soul's sake. (I:142)

Satan's attacks on the bodies of men and women, with the ultimate intention of damaging or destroying their souls, is a diabolical mirror of the work of Christ. Christ's mercy to people in healing their diseases is directed to the end of the healing of their souls—a sort of 'bribe', says Gurnall, that they might more willingly receive mercy for their souls from him who had been kind to their bodies. Gurnall compares it to training children, to whom are given something pleasing so they will do that which is less pleasing to them: as in 'go to school, learn their book'! (I:142— Gurnall should know; as already mentioned, he and Sarah had ten or more children.)

The devil is God's ape in his method; in this the Puritans again stand in the ancient Christian tradition. Satan imitates God; he is a 'copycat'.[39] As Christ is meek, the devil is cruel; and his cruelty to the body shows his plan for the soul as well. He is well aware of human enfleshment; he knows that body and soul are vitally interconnected. Distress to the body disturbs also the repose of the soul 'under whose very roof it dwells' (I:142). Thus the saints are vulnerable, and should not consider it strange if for lack of sleep

the tongue talk idly, so the soul should break out into some sinful carriage, which is the bottom of the devil's plot. (I:142)

Other people, experiencing distress brought on by the devil, are pushed by him into superstitious fear; and not only in areas of the world without the Gospel. Amongst his own contemporaries, Gurnall remarks there are many who, instead of seeking help and cure from God for their material and physical problems, turn to the devil and 'go . . . to his doctors—wizards I mean' (I:143).[40]

Yet, though the devil uses the body's frailty and vulnerability to illness, his access to the soul is not only through the body. Gurnall indicates that the devil, as a spirit, has access to the human spirit; and as a superior spirit, he has power over human beings as lower creatures. Gurnall goes so far as to say that the fall has actually allowed Satan, in some sense, to get 'within' the human soul (I:143). This closeness of access to the human heart Satan uses as God's imitator to emulate wickedly that which God does righteously. If God works effectually in the saints (Galatians 2:8), Satan works effectually in the children of disobedience (Ephesians 2:2). The Spirit enlightens, the devil 'blinds the minds of them which believe not' (2 Corinthians 4:4). The Holy Spirit fills the Christian; he comes with love, and is called the comforter (John 14:16, 17; Ephesians 5:18). Satan, in contrast, is a molester and a rapist. Gurnall uses a most striking image here, regarding

Judas, into whom it is said he entered, and when he had satisfied his lust upon him (as Amnon on Tamar), shuts the door of mercy upon him, and makes him that was even now traitor to his Master, hangman to himself. (I:143)

In attacking the human spirit, Gurnall says, the proper subjects of Satan's power are the unregenerate. Yet the saints are the chief objects of his wrath, and they are no match for the devil if God steps aside: 'He hath sent the strongest among them home, trembling and crying to their God' (I:143).

Despite the extensive exposition of Satan's power in the Puritans—by which they demonstrate their seriousness in this regard—they are at one in insisting on its limitedness. The devil's power is a derived power, and only a derived power. Gurnall says:

Satan's power is limited, and that two ways—he cannot do what he will, and he shall not do what he can. (I:146)

The devil's power is not infinite, but is curbed by God's all-ruling providence. John Downame shows how the infinite power of God turns the devil's works literally inside out:

He is indeed most malitiouslie disposed against the Lord, and by this his malice is stirred up to doe those things which he thinketh most displeasant in God's eies: but because the Lord chaineth and curbeth him in with his omnipotent power, he is onely able to doe those things that God permitteth him, and, will he nill he, he is constrained to obey his Creator and to be at his commandment.[41]

RULERS OF THE DARKNESS OF THIS WORLD
The Puritans take Paul's third category, 'rulers of the darkness of this world,' as specifying the proper seat of Satan's empire. This includes a threefold limitation: time, place, and subjects (I:148).[42]

First, the devil's rule is limited as to time: this world (life), not the hereafter. Gurnall here defines 'world' as that time which, like an inconsiderable parenthesis, is clapped in on either side with vast eternity (I:148); 'this present world', as the apostle calls it (Titus 2:12).

Using an image from the world of the theatre, Gurnall says that on this temporary stage, the devil as a mock king plays his part. But when at the end Christ comes to take down the scaffolding, the play will be over—the devil's crown removed, his 'sword broke over his head, and he hissed off with scorn and shame' (I:148). Thus, says William Gouge, 'At the end of this world shall Christ put downe his authoritie and power.'[43]

Matthew 9:29 indicates that the devils are aware of their time limitation, as is demonstrated by the question they ask when confronted by Jesus:

And, behold, they cried out, saying, What have we to do with thee, Jesus, thou Son of God? art thou come hither to torment us before the time? (I:148)

John Downame, who also draws attention to this time limitation, urges that this very limitation spurs the devil in his 'desperate and audacious' attacks on God and God's people,

for Satan, knowing that his time is but short, will redouble all his forces to work our destruction, even as soldiers will most fiercely assault a town, when as they cannot lie long at the siege . . .[44]

Second, the devil's rule is limited as to place: this world, not heaven. As a vagabond, excommunicated from heaven, Satan has no influence there.[45] He must thus content himself with working mischief here, bothering the saints on their way to the place where they will be finally and forever out of his reach (I:150). This knowledge is for Gurnall a great cause for joy. The saints' final goal, where their everlasting happiness lies, is safe forever from the devil's meddling. The Christian heart is already with Christ in heaven, Christian friends and relatives as well; the plots and snares of Satan encountered on the journey there will not affect the final outcome. Therefore, despite the suffering and failure a saint may experience here at the devil's hands, the enemy can never disturb the treasure a Christian has under safekeeping in heaven:

He cannot null thy faith, make void thy relation, dry up thy comfort . . . ; nor [can he] hinder thee a happy issue of thy whole war with sin, . . . these all are kept in heaven, among God's own crown-jewels, . . . (I:150, 151)

Third, the devil's rule is limited as to subjects, which the Puritans all agree are those human beings referred to by (or as) the 'darkness of this world'. Gurnall interprets 'darkness' in two ways, maintaining that it refers to sin in general, and to the sin of ignorance in particular. And the sense will be that the devil's rule is over those that are in a state of sin or ignorance, not over those who are sinful or ignorant (I:151).

Christians are both sinful and ignorant, and yet not in a state of sin and ignorance. Gurnall thus says that Christians are no longer under Satan's dominion; those who have not received God's mercy in Christ are subject to the devil in a most profound and total way (I:151).

Regarding the darkness of sin in general, each soul existing in a state of sin is under the devil's rule. Paul Bayne writes:

Whosoever do live in the state of darkness, they are under the devil's power. These are joined, the one as the foundation of the other; and before we have deliverance from the one, we cannot be freed from the other.[46]

Darkness in the soul is the source of sin—as when Jesus said of those who crucified him 'they know not what they do': 'We may say when anyone sins, he doth he knows not what' (I:151). This darkness is a kind of moral and spiritual blindness within each person, but not such as releases men and women from responsibility. It is a wilful blindness, as expressed in the old saying 'There are none so blind as those who will not see.' This self-willed spiritual blindness is the primary internal cause of sin; Satan is the promoter, the external cause. In this state:

All the sinner's apprehensions of things are shaped by Satan; he looks on sin with the devil's spectacles, he reads the word with the devil's comment, he sees nothing in its native colours, but is under a continual delusion. (I:153)

Sin is not only darkness within the soul; it also brings darkness into the soul. It is self-reinforcing, and 'progress' in sin can be said to increase the darkness. Gurnall uses the example of that substance which, when tasted, affects the sense of taste so that one can no longer distinguish sweet from bitter. So with the person who at one time could see a certain sin as absurd and disgusting in others:

When once he hath drunk off this enchanting cup himself—as one that hath foredone his understanding—is mad of it himself, not able now to see the evil of it, or use his reason against it. (I:152)

The darkness of this state of sin has also a judicial aspect; it is part of God's judgment on rebellion against the truth. Paul in the first chapter of his epistle to the Romans says that one consequence of the suppression of truth is God's 'giving over' of humanity to believe a lie. This state of affairs is also self-reinforcing; rebellion brings judicial darkening. Further progress in the practice of sin causes the sinner to actively seek the darkness. A sort of downward spiral occurs, a 'descent into the abyss'. Gurnall describes the duplicity that begins to characterize such a person:

So in moral wickedness, sinners like beasts go out in the night for their prey, loath to be seen, afraid to come where they should be found out. Nothing more terrible to sinners than [the] light of truth, because their deeds are evil, John 3:19. (I:152)

Those under the rule of the prince of darkness, in this general state of sin, are called in 1 John 3:10 the children of the devil. Again, in Matthew 12:44, they are called the household of the devil. An individual in this state is enslaved; Satan rules the whole person: the thinking is shaped by him, the will effectually controlled, the person's time is used for his concerns. When the call of God comes to attend to spiritual things, to pray, to heed the Scripture, such a person just cannot find the time. But

if the sinner hears there is a merry-meeting, a knot of good fellows at the alehouse, all is thrown aside to wait on his lord and master . . . , wife and children crying, may be starving; while the wretch is pouring out their very blood, in wasting their livelihood, at the foot of his lust. (I:154)

The final outcome of remaining in this state of darkness is exactly that: it leads to final and utter darkness, an irrevocable state where sin and torment become permanent and inextinguishable:

Hell-birds are no changelings, their torment makes them sin, and their sin feeds their torment, both unquenchable, one being fuel to another. (I:153)

'Darkness', according to Gurnall and many of the other

Puritans, also refers specifically to the sin of ignorance, which 'above other sins enslaves a soul to Satan' (I:161). William Gouge says that darkness refers to wicked and ignorant men, with 'no light of spiritual understanding.'

For souls characterized by such spiritual ignorance, 'The Devill is said to be the god of them that are blinded.'[47] Paul Bayne sounds the same note. Commenting on darkness as ignorance, he says 'ignorance is the very foundation of the devil's kingdom.'[48]

This ignorance, as distinct from the 'blindness' spoken of as a general state of darkness and sin, is specifically meant by the Puritans to refer to lack of instruction. Without thorough teaching of the biblical revelation, people have uninformed minds and consciences. The person who is ignorant of spiritual reality, ignorant of God (as well as of the enemy of God) is undone. Such a one is absolutely open and unguarded, defenceless before the onslaught of the devil. Gurnall uses an illustration reminiscent of John Bunyan's *Holy War*:

Ignorance opens the door for Satan to enter with his troops of lusts. Where the watch is blind, the city is soon taken. An ignorant man sins, and like drunken Lot, he knows not when the tempter comes, . . . (I:161)

The Puritans all believe that ignorance, contrary to being a blissful state ('ignorance is bliss'), is a most lamentable condition. Effectively disarming one against attack, and opening the door to welcome the enemy, ignorance also locks the soul in sin once it has entered: 'Ignorance lays the soul asleep under the hatches of stupidity' (I:162).

The conscience, says Gurnall, is the alarm of God to call up the sinner; but in an ignorant soul, conscience is silent.

It is only active when it has been informed, as conscience can only be a witness to that which it knows (I:162). A beast instinctively avoids that which endangers it. Human beings, says Gurnall, being nobler, have been given a double guard: natural fear of danger, and natural shame of wrongdoing. Both of these are silent in an ignorant soul. The ignorant man

sins and blusheth not, because he knows not his guilt; . . . Neither is he afraid, because he knows not his danger; and therefore he plays with his sin, as the child with the waves, that, by and by, will swallow him up. (I:162)

Deprived of natural fear and shame, men and women sin with impunity.

The Puritans thus see moral relativism as a species of ignorance, the darkness of this world, the work of the rulers of that darkness. More than relativism—sometimes seen as tolerance—the Puritans show that satanic ignorance actually constitutes an inversion: evil becomes good, dark light. Richard Gilpin in his *Daemonologia Sacra* illustrates this in a striking critique of power. He writes that Satan's power of darkening the mind is graphically shown in the inversion of values that accompanies worldly power. Gilpin notes how the mighty of the world strut about in great pomp and pride, parading their accomplishments for all to admire. Yet often these 'accomplishments' have meant the destruction of cities and kingdoms, the spilling of blood of millions. Commenting on the 'new-speak' of his own day, Gilpin points out how these exploits are often given the names of 'virtue, manhood, courage, magnanimity, conquest.' He says better they should be called by their proper names of cruelty, murder, robbery, and so on.[49] Thus spiritual ignorance turns things into their opposites.

Not only are natural fear and shame silent when people are ignorant; the devil himself (to his delight) is dismissed as innocuous. Gouge says such folk see no need to resist the devil, as they are unaware of his great power, malice, and deception. They do not believe that the devil is such a bad fellow; in fact,

they thinke him to be the best Lord, because he suffereth them to doe as they list, and his temptations are agreeable to their corrupt humours and carnall desires.[50]

Ignorance also shuts out hope of recovery. Not perceiving the true situation, the soul does not respond to promises or threats. Some paths seem right to a traveller, but only lead back to where one began:

After many years travel, as they think, towards heaven by their good meanings, blind devotions, and reformation, when they shall expect to be within sight of heaven, they shall find themselves even where they were at first, as very slaves to Satan as ever. (I:162)

Gurnall's description here sounds very like John Bunyan's portrayal of the character Ignorance in *The Pilgrim's Progress*. Ignorance travels—as he thinks—toward the heavenly city, blissfully ignorant and unaware of his own doom right to the moment of judgment.[51] It is truly an awful picture; ignorant persons are Satan's tame slaves, 'as the silly sheep before the butcher' (I:163), standing in the devil's presence not knowing who their master is.

SPIRITUAL WICKEDNESS IN HIGH PLACES

Paul's fourth category, 'spiritual wickedness in high places,' Gurnall renders literally 'the spirituals of wickedness.' He understands this to mean the spiritual nature of the devils and the wickedness of that nature, as well as the spiritual sins to which the devils vigorously tempt the saints:

The spirituals of wickedness, not those gross fleshly sins, which the herd of beastly sinners, like swine, wallow in, but sin spiritualized, . . . (I:176)

Gurnall first discusses the spiritual nature of the devils. In terms of their actual existence, the devils are spirits, evil angels, not flesh; in the terminology of modern parapsychology, they are 'discarnate entities'.[52] In essence, devils are immaterial and simple, not compounded of matter and spirit like human beings. Gurnall quotes Jesus' own statement to this effect from Luke 24:39:

'Handle me and see,' saith Christ to his disciples, that thought they had seen a spirit, 'for a spirit hath not flesh and bones, as ye see me have.' (I:177)

This immateriality allows the devils entry 'into' bodies, as in the case of the man possessed by a legion of devils (Luke 8:30); bodies cannot merge into other bodies (I:177).

The Puritans, in unity with most other Christians throughout history (at least until very recently), believe that devils are spiritual substances, unbodied intelligences, which exist independently of human beings; they have actual, objective existence. Richard Gilpin mentions the fact that in his time, there are those who think 'that our own fancies or imaginations may be the only devils that vex us.'[53] Gurnall is very emphatic: the devils are 'not qualities, or evil motions, arising from us, as some have absurdly conceived.'[54] Beginning with the Sadducees in Jesus' own time, Gurnall notes that this view has existed right up to his own day:[55] and to him its ancient pedigree qualifies it as one amongst many other 'bad old ideas':

But this is so fond a conceit, that, to maintain it, we must forfeit our reason and deny the Scriptures. (I:177)[56]

For Gurnall and the other Puritans, it is both reasonable and Scriptural to believe in the actual existence of devils. In fact, not to do so is mad. For the Puritans, the evidence points to the undeniable conclusion that spirits of evil exist and are active.

Gurnall briefly examines the Scriptural evidence regarding the creation (Colossians 1:16), fall (Jude 6) and destiny of the evil angels, as well as their present evil work. He takes this evidence as sufficient to establish the fact, but observes that

so immersed is sorry man in flesh, that he will not easily believe what he sees not with his fleshly eyes. Upon the same account we may deny the being of God himself, because invisible. (I:177)

These spiritual beings, though finite, remain awesome enemies to humanity in several respects. Their vastness of intellect is immeasurably greater than the human mind; they have 'subtilty too much for all the saints on earth, if we had not a God to play our game for us' (I:178).

Being spirits, they also have the advantage of invisibility. 'We to spirits are as blind men,' says Gouge.[57] As their presence is undetectable to the eye, so their assaults come without warning. Human consciousness tends to be dominated by that which is most immediately present to the senses, which gives the devils great advantage. 'Out of sight, out of mind' applies in this case. Gurnall observes that people fear apparitions, 'things that go bump in the night'; yet they carry the devil within 'their hearts, and walk all day long in his company, and fear him not' (I:178). They have the inside track on whatever we do or say, notes Gouge, daylight or dark, alone or in company.[58]

The Puritans also mention the mobility of angels as a factor that again puts humans at a distinct disadvantage. In his *Christian Warfare*, John Downame comments that the devils can move with incredible swiftness from one place to others 'which are farre distant'; they can attack at their pleasure, or withdraw if resisted to await a more opportune time. He describes that which gives every child (and many adults) nightmares:

Being spirits they can lie secretly in ambushment, even in our bedchambers, and so surprize us when they find us most retchlesse and secure.[59]

The Puritans teach that the wicked spirits never tire, another obvious advantage. Gurnall comments that when human beings are at war, weariness often sets in: 'the conqueror must sit down and breathe, and so loseth the chase' (I:178).

Not so with the devils. Gouge explains that weariness, failure, and decay obtain amongst human beings because of their material frame. The devils, being simple spirit, do not experience these things:

Hence it is, that after they have done many thousand great exploits, they are as fresh and ready to doe many more, as they were at first. They need no resting time, but continually, night and day are assaulting men without intermission, and without ceasing.[60]

The final point, in regard to the fallen angels' purely spiritual existence, is that they are immortal spirits. As they do not weary, neither do they die, and this makes them even more terrible as enemies. The most dreadful opponent on earth eventually will die, as Gurnall says:

Persecuting men walk a turn or two upon the stage, and are called off by death, and there is an end of all their plots. (I:178)

In contrast, the devils live on: 'they will hunt thee to thy grave,' and Gurnall believes they will meet the wicked in another world to accuse and torment them there as well (I:178).[61]

Their deathlessness has also given them the advantage of thousands of years of experience in tempting human beings; this gathering of experience is often mentioned by the Puritans. Each new generation of saints must meet an enemy of great antiquity and age upon age of collected experience. The devils have had plenty of time to develop their craft to a fine perfection.[62]

The devils exist as spiritual beings; but the spirituality of their nature is depraved beyond knowing. They are inconceivably wicked.[63] Their wickedness as fallen creatures is commensurate with the nobility of their creation, as angels created so near to God himself. Satan's rebellion is therefore all the more despicable, because of the height of the position he first occupied. Every advantage was his; he was the 'peer and favourite' of the court of heaven, and 'to make this bold and blasphemous attempt to snatch at God's own crown, this paints the devil blacker than the thoughts of men and angels can conceive' (I:179).

Thus Satan, and the angels who rebelled with him, became the inventors of sin—the first to blow the trumpet of rebellion, leaders of the dance of sin from the beginning. 'And this is a dreadful aggravation, that they sinned without a tempter' (I:179).[64]

Though human beings, says Gurnall, are not capable of sin of this degree, some sin similarly to the devils, in that they invent evil things (Romans 1:30). Gurnall observes that in each generation there are those who become infamous, making 'old sins new by superadding to the wickedness of others.' For example:

Uncleanness is an old sin from the beginning; but the Sodomites will be filthy in a new way, and therefore it carries their name to this day. (I:179)

Originality in sin, say the Puritans, is a devilish hallmark.

The spiritual wickedness of the fallen angels is seen in their primary activity in the world, which is the tempting of men and women to sin (I:179). The devils' multiple costumes, their shifting, 'now you see 'em, now you don't' approaches to humans, their dissembling and deceiving methods, all are directed toward the end of drawing human beings to evil, and thence to destruction. Their intention is always the same, whether they approach people directly, or through various instruments: 'the Flesh, the World, Persecutors, Idolaters, Heretikes, profane men, etc.'[65]

Gouge maintains that whenever men or women are solicited to evil, the devil is at their elbow; if they capitulate, he has in fact beguiled them and prevailed over them.[66] Paul Bayne feels that the godly can even become possessed 'after a sort' if they consent to a demonic temptation.[67] This 'possession' is not identical with the total demonization found amongst people without Christ. Rather, Bayne says:

The godly, when they give place to him, they let him come into the suburbs and outparts; but because Christ dwelleth in their hearts by faith, the tower being kept, he is, by the renewing of their faith and repentance, forced to retire.[68]

The spiritual nature of the devils is immutably and untiringly fixed on evil, and particularly on dragging human beings into evil. This engagement in wickedness, this fixation upon doing only evil continually—what energizes it? William Gouge suggests that 'he is most willing and forward unto evill, taking delight therein.'[69] Richard Baxter uses the same word—delight—to describe the wickedness of spirits who 'delight to do Mischief, and that lye and deceive Men.'[70] Whether by 'delight' they actually mean the devil receives enjoyment from his wicked work is open to question, as such 'enjoyment' would be of a diabolical nature. Yet it is observable in human life that humans do get pleasure of a sort from evil—thus our word 'sadistic', to cite only one well-known example. So it is conceivable that the Puritans understand the devil to take a nefarious pleasure in his destructive work.

Gurnall, however, seems to back away from saying the devil gains pleasure or delight in attacking human beings.

When he draws souls to sin, it is not because he tastes any sweetness or finds any profit therein—he hath too much light to have any joy or peace in sin. (I:180)

Rather, says Gurnall, the devil is possessed of malice, a

desire to see souls damned, that amounts to a sort of pathological fury, a demented rage. Hatred is what energizes the devil and his angels, hatred toward God first of all. Gurnall says the devil hates God with

a perfect hatred; and because he cannot reach him with a direct blow, therefore he strikes him at the second hand through his saints; . . . well knowing the life of God is in a manner bound up in theirs. (I:180, 181)

The action of the devil toward the saints, then, is like a mad dog attacking a flock of sheep. The dog does not kill to eat, it simply kills to kill (I:180). In like manner, the devil attacks the saints, consumed with hatred for them and for their God.

Malice as descriptive of the satanic wickedness appears very often in the other Puritans. Thomas Watson, in fact, collates malice with delight, and seems to see them as one and the same:

This hellish serpent is swelled with the poison of malice. . . . If there be anything this infernal spirit can delight in, it is to ruin souls, . . . This malice of Satan in tempting must needs be great, . . .[71]

Baxter and Gouge may in fact be saying the same thing: malice or hatred is the devil's delight. John Downame also emphasizes the depth of Satan's malice, indicating that it is nearly as ancient as the world itself, and that it will last forever. He describes the great red dragon

who is so flesht in bloud and crueltie, and so overcaried with malice and hatred, that he esteemeth it his chiefe sport and pastime to destroy us.[72]

Notice how Downame assimilates 'malice and hatred' to

the devil's 'chiefe sport and pastime.' He seems to be making the same point as Watson does in bringing malice and delight together. But John Downame thinks the devil's malice derives partly from envy. He is jealous of the 'love and favour of God toward the faithfull.'[73] William Bridge, another slightly older contemporary of William Gurnall, in his third sermon on temptation also speaks of Satan's malice rooted in envy. The devil cannot bear to hear the Lord honouring his children, says Bridge; he becomes envious:

And when he hears any of God's children triumphing by faith, and making boast of the love of God, then does his malice kindle into a flame; Shall such a one go to heaven, and shall I be damned, . . .[74]

Thus the Puritans depict the spiritual wickedness of the fallen angels: a nightmare picture of beings driven by a consuming envy for that which they can never acquire, malevolent to the very core, expressing malice toward everything, but particularly toward God and his people.

William Gurnall, ever the pastor, wants his hearers to see how this horror of spiritual wickedness applies to their own lives. He holds up the mirror of satanic wickedness as it reflects human nature. Gurnall admits it is difficult to get a good look at human nature in its wholeness. People often find it hard to conceive of human nature as desperately wicked, because they see only the stream of above-ground, external or surface sins, which may seem quite small. They do not see the immensity of the subterranean fountain that incessantly feeds the stream. Gurnall wants his hearers, by observing the wickedness of the devils, to see the potential for wickedness in their own hearts:

Thou art not yet fledged, thy wings are not grown to make thee a flying dragon; but thou art of the same brood, the seed of the serpent is in thee, and the devil begets a child like himself. . . . None but Christ can give thee a new heart, till which thou wilt every day grow worse and worse. Sin is an hereditary disease that increaseth with age. A young sinner shall be an old devil. (I:181)

Regarding the meaning of Paul's phrase concerning the location or sphere of operation of these wicked spirits, 'in high places', the Puritans are not of one mind. Paul Bayne understands it in a fairly literal sense, that the devils are 'in high places, are above us. . . . these spiritual wickednesses hang hovering over our heads'.[75] Baxter holds a similar viewpoint: 'it seems that they dwell near us, in the Air, Earth and Sea, and not in the higher glorious Regions.'[76] William Gurnall, while not agreeing with this interpretation, yet says 'Indeed this way most interpreters go' (I:213).[77]

The idea is that the devils hover closely about and above, spying, watching human behaviour from this elevated vantage point in order to find fault. Bayne therefore says that since

we lie naked to the view of them, we must be careful that they spy nothing in us to their advantage. . . . , wherefore we had need be circumspect . . .[78]

The image is very like that of an invisible peeping tom (or many peeping toms), but instead of peering through a window, these spiritual voyeurs hover about invisibly, leering and looking over every move in order to find an opportunity to tempt or accuse.

Another Puritan view of 'high places', or 'the heavenlies', sees this as a metaphor referring simply to the superior position and advantage possessed by the devil. John Calvin had commented on this passage:

Nor do these words countenance the belief that the devil has created and keeps for himself the middle region of the air. Paul does not assign to them a fixed territory, which they hold and control, but merely indicates that they are engaged in hostility, and are higher in place.[79]

John Downame follows the Reformer here. Paul's statement that the devils are in high places shows that they have 'gotten the advantage of the upper ground.' The enemy thus has tactical superiority, and the fight will obviously be dangerous:

when an enemy fighteth against us from an high place or fort, we standing so low that we are scarce able to reach them.[80]

William Gouge and William Gurnall express a third view. Both writers note the adjective 'heavenlies' stands alone, translators having supplied places (I:213).[81] Gouge's own judgment is that the apostle is referring to 'heavenly things'—that is, that the warfare between the Christian and the devil is over heavenly things: whether one will serve the heavenly Father or the hellish fiend.[82] Gurnall here agrees with Gouge. He contends that the New Testament usage of 'heavenlies' is not in reference to aerial places,

but always for things truly heavenly and spiritual. The word, indeed, properly signifies supercelestial, and if applied to places, would signify that where the devil never came since his fall. (I:214)

Gurnall argues that superiority of place may give some advantage to human beings over their enemies (I:214), but is meaningless applied to spiritual enemies.

As Gurnall interprets it, Christians wrestle against the 'spirituals of wickedness' for the heavenly prize. The world is extrinsic, a stranger to the Christian, 'and intermeddles not with his joy or grief' (I:214). Christians, if they have put off the world, are not much attacked by the devil over worldly things—'this were as if one should think to hurt a man by beating of his clothes when he hath put them off' (I:214).

The attacks of the devil upon Christians are more directed to heavenly treasure. Christians, being the offspring of God, are made heavenly and holy by that relationship. The wicked spirit's goal, says Gurnall, is to 'debase and deflower this' (I:214; note again the reference to the devil as a rapist). The devil's malice, powered by envy, is shown in that he attacks precisely the attribute of the Christian that he himself has lost:

He hath lost that beauty of holiness which once shone so gloriously on his angelical nature; and now, like a true apostate, he endeavours to ruin that in the Christian which he hath lost himself. (I:214)

Thus the Puritans display the enemy of God and of his saints. The Christian life being a combat, they also want Christians to know their own vulnerabilities and weaknesses, so they may be prepared to face such an enemy. Christian vulnerability to attack is discussed in the next chapter.

3

The Embattled Christian: Vulnerability to Attack

The Puritan description of the devil, sketched in the last chapter, is not done for its own sake. The Puritans have no interest in the devil for himself, as some who are obsessed with things evil and occult out of unhealthy curiosity. Rather, the Puritans' interest is pastoral: they teach and write to equip the saints, so they will not be ignorant of the enemy of their souls and of his devices.

The Puritan writers go beyond description of the devils, to describe the vulnerability of the saints. They wish to warn Christians of their weaknesses in the face of such powerful and ruthless enemies, to impart to them an accurate self-understanding. 'Well knew the Apostle,' writes William Gouge, 'that the best Christians, while here they live in this world, are both prone to faint by reason of their own weaknesse, and also in hazard to be foiled by reason of their enemies power.'

THE NEW CREATURE AND INDWELLING SIN

The Puritans teach that a Christian is a 'new creature' (2 Corinthians 5:17). Yet the Christian life is not one of ease and glory. Rather, the Puritans depict a life of continual struggle; not only of struggle, but nevertheless a life which will include much conflict (Bunyan's *Pilgrim's Progress* has given powerful literary form to this conception). The primary source of this conflict is the legacy of original sin: evil has taken up residence in the human soul. The Westminster Confession, speaking of the primal disobedience of the first human pair, says:

By this sin they fell from their original righteousness, and communion with God, and so became dead in sin, and wholly defiled in all the faculties and parts of soul and body. They being the root of all mankind, the guilt of this sin was imputed, and the same death in sin and corrupted nature conveyed to all their posterity, descending from them by ordinary generation. From this original corruption, whereby we are utterly indisposed, disabled, and made opposite to all good, and wholly inclined to all evil, do proceed all actual transgressions.[1]

The Puritans understand evil as lying at the heart of each human person, a fundamental warping of motivation, desire, and choice that turns the heart away from its true source and end, God, and directs it onto itself and the creation. This condition is permanent unless a person experiences the transformation of a new birth, something which only the grace of God can effect. Regeneration causes a radical change at the heart of human personality, turning it back toward God. This, however, is just the beginning. Following the new birth, the remainder of one's earthly life is taken up with the growth and nurture of this new life. It does not grow automatically, as if mechanically.

There reside within the Christian remnants of original sin which are still active (see Note 4), and which must be put to death, or as the Puritans say, mortified. Gurnall's contemporary, John Owen, writes his treatises on sin and temptation to deal specifically with this internal warfare.[2] The Westminster Confession describes it this way:

This corruption of nature, during this life, doth remain in those that are regenerated: and although it be through Christ pardoned and mortified, yet both itself, and all the motions thereof, are truly and properly sin.[3]

It is perhaps a modern conceit to think that only in this century have Christians understood that God's work has both present and future aspects, both the 'now' and the 'not yet'; for this is precisely the notion held by the Puritans in regard to the Christian life. Regeneration has brought about a fundamental reordering, at the deepest level, of the human personality; love for God has been restored, where once there was only fear and hatred. Yet indwelling sin, though crucified, is able to struggle still. The growth of the new creature takes all the rest of the Christian's earthly life, as does the death of sin. The Christian life is the working out of this conflict, in which more and more of the old personality orientation-to-self-as-god is exposed and put to death, while the new life grows progressively stronger, more mature, more dominant. But the Christian arrives at perfection only when face to face with God in the world to come; perfection is not attainable while still in the fallen world.[4]

This portrait of the Christian life strongly informs the Puritan presentation of spiritual warfare. Within the regenerated person is the battle against sin, but this conflict is exacerbated by the presence of Satan and his hosts, and their attacks. So Christians must deal with both their own sinful tendencies, and the invisible enemies who seek to seduce, to distract, to frighten, to hinder; who seek to facilitate the expression of sin still remaining in them, 'according to their natures, constitutions, complexions, ages, sexes, etc.'[5]

This major theme of Christian vulnerability is expounded from many angles by William Gurnall and the other Puritans; a few of these are surveyed in this chapter.

WEAKNESS OF THE CHRISTIAN'S SANCTIFYING GRACE

William Gurnall speaks of the weakness of the Christian's grace, that is, weakness in the area of one's sanctification, in one's growth in holiness and likeness to Christ. A saint's falling short of perfection in this life entails weakness—if not in all points, yet in some. Gurnall describes the Christian as

a weak creature conflicting with enemies stronger than itself, and therefore cannot keep the field without an auxiliary strength from heaven. (I:21)

The principle of grace in a new Christian has been planted there by God, through conquest; it is like a newly planted colony, unwelcome to the native residents. Thus the Christian's first enemies are those that dwell within, the corruptions of indwelling sin. These are ready to creep out of the dens where they lurk, to eat up the new creature (I:21). John Downame details the weaknesses of the Christian's grace, having to contend with such inner enemies:

These graces are . . . but weakened and imperfect in us; our truth being mixt with wil-worship and hypocrisie; the puritie of our conscience being stained with our corruption; our knowledge of the Gospell but in part, . . . ; our faith mixt with doubting, . . . ; our hope shaken from our anker-hold, when the promises of God are delaied . . .[6]

This weakness means the devil can carry on with less trouble than he would receive from a stronger opponent (as when he tried to tempt Jesus in the wilderness).[7] Thus while the new creature resists the devil, the concupiscence remaining welcomes him. Bayne pictures indwelling sin as a sort of harlot of the soul, receptive to the attractions of illicit lovers: 'For the most part our lust is moved and excited by these spirits; they blow the coals up, and are the sires of the sin whereof our concupiscence is the mother.'[8] Christians are vulnerable all their lives. The Puritans do not believe any saint, no matter how advanced, can go toe-to-toe with the devil and prevail:

Yea, he would soon make an end of the war in the ruin of the believer's grace, did not Heaven take the Christian into protection. (I:21)

While the Puritans teach that all Christians are in need of God's sustaining grace until they die—and are thus always 'weak' creatures—they do not then excuse Christians from the duty to strengthen and to exert themselves. The fact that the saints are weak and needy creatures is never an excuse for laziness or lack of effort in Christian living. Quite the opposite. Puritan teaching is noteworthy for the demands it places on all Christians, no matter their age, sex, station or ability. As regenerated people, with the divine life newly planted and growing within them, all believers are to exert themselves to the fullest of their powers. Lack of perfection should not lead to passivity or paralysis. Baxter says:

But seeing it is the free will of Man that giveth the Devils their hurting power, and they can do us no harm, nor make us sin, without our own consent and yielding: O! With how careful and constant and resolved watchfulness should we live?[9]

Thus Gurnall says that Christians are to exercise their grace; if they do not, they endanger not only themselves, but others as well (passivity, instead of decreasing vulnerability, increases it). An irresponsible weakness due to neglect endangers one's family. The Puritans powerfully argue the need for holiness in parents. Heads of families must exert themselves strenuously, recognizing the needs of their children:

If thy heart be in a holy frame, they fare the better in the duties thou performest; if thy heart be dead and down, they are losers by the hand. So that as the nurse eats the more for the babe's sake she suckles, so shouldst thou for their sake who are under thy tuition, be more careful to exercise thy own grace, and cherish it. (I:66)

An irresponsible weakness also endangers the church. This outward look is characteristic of the Puritans. Those who think the Puritans advocate navel-gazing introspection, a sort of negative spiritual narcissism (always gazing inward in hope of finding more sin) misunderstand the movement. What internal self-examination they advocate is to end in going outward again to meet God, or to act on behalf of others. The Puritan life is not exclusively oriented to oneself, and concern over one's own spirituality. It is rather both individual and communal. John

Downame, calling for prayers on behalf of the church, says:

For we are fellow members of the same bodie, we are fellow souldiers which fight under the same Captaine Jesus Christ, and consequently their victorie is our victorie, and their foiles are our foiles.[10]

The church is made up of individual Christians, and individual Christians together make up the church. There is no one-or-the-other, no exclusive focus on either extreme. When preaching to the individual Christian conscience, the Puritans are always speaking in the context of the church as the body, as the family of God.[11] In such a context, irresponsible and neglectful weakness is liable to cause damage to one's brothers and sisters:

We must keep grace in exercise in respect of others our fellow-soldiers. Paul had this in eye when he was exercising himself to keep a good conscience, that he might not be a scandal to others. . . . The ignorance of one soldier that hath not skill to handle his arms, may do mischief to his fellow-soldiers about him. (I:65)[12]

VULNERABILITY AT SPECIFIC TIMES
William Gurnall exercises a sort of spiritual psychology in pinpointing the times in the saints' lives when they are especially vulnerable to assault. In this he is at one with the other eminent Puritans, who make it their business to deal with living out the faith for a lifetime. Puritanism is realistic about human failure and sin, and the difficulty of living a holy life amidst these challenges. Yet that is the genius of the Puritan programme—spiritual rigour and determination to grow and prevail despite inevitable setbacks and disappointments. Puritan exercise of pastoral care is not

dependent upon ideal circumstances, but is worked out in the midst of the difficulties of seventeenth-century life.

The devil knows that human beings are more vulnerable at certain times than at others; in his strategy he shows himself to be a wily pragmatist. For the devil, the old slogan 'whatever works, is right' is true indeed.

Satan shows his black art, and hellish skill, in speaking words of seduction and temptation in season; and a word in season is a word on its wheels (I:72). Like an expert angler who knows when fish bite best, so the devil 'can hit the very joint of time' when his temptation is most effective.[13]

His craftiness is not the only devilish characteristic manifested in this way of attacking the saints. The Puritan view that the devil is a despicable coward crops up here, as John Downame says:

We are first to observe that it is most cruell and cowardly, for he observeth no complements of true valour, but then most violently assaulteth us when we are least provided; . . .[14]

Logically enough, Gurnall begins at the beginning. The newly converted Christian is a prime target of the devil (C. S. Lewis may have picked up a hint here; *Screwtape* starts similarly): 'The first cry of the new creature gives all the legions of hell an alarm' (I:72).[15] Greatly chagrined, the devils respond to conversion as King Herod did to the news of Jesus' birth (I:72). The Christian, newborn and inexperienced, has the gullibility of the young child and is thus an easy target. Conversion has put the new saint beyond the devil's grasp regarding final destiny—but not beyond temptation.

As new Christians are weak in knowledge, the devil seeketh to abuse their simplicitie, by drawing them either into errours and heresies, or at least into blind zeale and superstition.[16]

Weak also in the development of Christian character, both in the growth of Christian graces and the mortification of indwelling sin (I:72), the devil then labours to weigh the young saint down with guilt, 'and to plunge them into the bottomlesse gulfe of horrour and despaire'.[17] The Puritans, renowned for their pastoral wisdom, obviously have plenty of experience observing the volatile character of new converts: filled with overflowing zeal and love one moment, falling prey to pride and old habits the next.

Christians are also targets of the devil in times when things seem to be going very well indeed, during seasons of prosperity. The Puritans are unanimous in trumpeting long, loud warnings regarding prosperity. John Owen sees prosperity and temptation going hand-in-hand:

Yea, prosperity is a temptation, many temptations, . . . Blessed is he that feareth always, but especially in a time of prosperity.[18]

These Calvinists, contrary to some conceptions of them, certainly do not say that material prosperity is a sign of election or of God's blessing. Thomas Watson says human beings usually handle adversity better than prosperity:

A prosperous condition is not always so safe. True it is more pleasing to the palate, and every one desires to get on the warm side of the hedge, where the sun of prosperity shines, but it is not always best; . . . Prosperity breeds pride. . . . Prosperity breeds security.[19]

The Puritans have a deep sense that worldly security often brings with it spiritual insecurity, and that wealth makes

one vulnerable to the devil. Prosperity can lead to an elevated view of one's own importance (and thus a lowering of
one's view of God); the devil can lead a wealthy saint to a
misplaced dependence on material things. As well, the
church is at risk, since it contains both poor and rich.
Downame says the devil takes advantage of prosperity,
tempting the church to contempt for its poorer members,
to a love for worldly things, to coldness in religion:

For he will persuade us, how wickedly soever we live, that we are
highlie in God's favour, otherwise he would not bestow so great
and manifold benefits upon us, as paunes and pledges of his
love.[20]

Puritan methodology often entails looking at a particular issue, then turning to its opposite. Thus in this case:
another season when the saints are particularly likely to be
assaulted is in the midst of affliction, which may come
from a number of sources. Gurnall mentions Job, and
Jesus during his forty day fast in the wilderness, as
examples (I:73). As in his attacks on new believers, the
devil is revealed in his cowardice as a monstrous molester,
attacking those weaker than himself at their weakest
points.

Affliction may come to the saints in the form of severe
persecution, where Satan comes as a lion in order to scare
Christians from the truth. Gurnall says that the first man
murdered was a saint—and he was killed for religion.
'And as Luther said, Cain will kill Abel unto the end of the
world' (I:304). Richard Gilpin, who once again displays a
remarkable feeling for the injustice imposed upon the
weak by those in power, reflects upon Satan's fury and
cruelty in the brutal persecutions that have taken place:

If we withal consider what inventions and devices of cruelty and torture he hath found out, and what endless variety of pains and miseries he hath prepared, . . . we can do no less than wonder at the merciless fury and implacable rage of him that contrived them.[21]

Adversity often takes the form of physical illness and pain, or the loss of material goods. Downame points out, and Gurnall after him (I:73), that Satan will use such afflictions to persuade the saints to fall into unbelief, turning from trust and dependence on God to unlawful remedies.[22] The devil will try to convince the saints that the way to relief is through the sin he is presenting. Thus, for the impoverished saint,

Satan comes, What! wilt starve rather than step over the hedge and steal for thy supply? This is enough to put flesh and blood to the stand. (I:73)[23]

Death is the final affliction, and the Puritans agree that at the hour of death, when the Christian is physically spent, 'now this coward falls upon him' (I:74). Now or never; the devil knows the game is nearly over, and he seeks to snatch dying saints for himself, or else make their going as miserable as possible (I:74). How well this accords with Bunyan's account of Christian's crossing of the River of Death. Despondent at such a prospect, yet seeing there is no other way to the gates of the City, Christian goes with Hopeful into the water, whereupon Christian immediately begins to sink. A

great darkness and horror fell upon Christian, so that he could not see before him; . . . 'Twas also observed that he was troubled with apparitions of hobgoblins and evil spirits, . . .[24]

Along with such manifestations, Christian fears he will die in the River and not find entrance to the City; thoughts of his sins plague him, and he fears God has abandoned him. Hopeful encourages Christian, and he finally regains his confidence in Christ. Bunyan then names the source of Christian's despair:

Then they both took courage, and the Enemy was after that as still as a stone, until they were gone over.[25]

In his *Body of Divinity*, Watson uses another striking image, drawn from sheep farming, to make the same point. As crows will peck at a weak and sickly sheep that cannot defend itself, so,

when a saint is weak on his deathbed, the devil pecks at him with a temptation. He reserves his most furious assaults till the last.[26]

Surely this conviction accounts, at least in part, for the strong Puritan emphasis on the need to prepare to die well. Richard Gilpin observes that it is Satan's work to rob the dying of their peace and joy, and to fill them with fear. Approaching death can cause great despondency, he says, unless the saints 'have great assurance of salvation, and have well learned to die'.[27]

Pleasure presents another area of potential weakness for Christians. The devil knows how to lure into sin when an object of desire is nearby (the Puritans could have been anticipating the late twentieth-century Western church in this regard). This approach is as old as the Garden of Eden, says Gurnall, when the serpent tempted Eve. Lust in the heart of the Christian is dangerous enough in itself, doubly so when the object of that lust is near to hand. The Christian is therefore in a most critical position if overly self-confident, and careless regarding exposure to sources of temptation.

If the Christian can let the object come so near, Satan will promise himself [that] his suit may in time be granted. . . . Look not on that beauty with a wandering eye, by which thou wouldst not be taken prisoner. (I:74)

Watson juxtaposes this manner of temptation with times of idleness in the Christian's life. The old saying 'Idle hands are the devil's workshop' applies here. King David was walking on the housetop unemployed, 'the devil set a tempting object before him, and it prevailed.'[28]

Dangerous temptations are also present at times when Christians engage in 'good works':

When the Christian is about some notable enterprise for God's glory, then Satan will lie like a serpent in the way. (I:73)

Paul Bayne gives a salient warning: Satan is not necessarily opposed to good works. On the contrary, he can actually be behind them, encouraging the saint to keep busy, if by so doing he can 'jostle out a better work, or . . . draw in with that good some greater evil.'[29] The more public these good works (the ubiquitous 'ministry' in our day), the greater the danger, the greater the devil's opportunity to wreak astonishing havoc, in individual Christian lives, as well as in families, the church, and the world at large.

Luke, in Acts 15:36–40, records that Paul and Barnabas, intending to visit the new churches to encourage them, fall into disagreement, and 'grow so hot that they part in this storm' (I:73). Though the text does not specifically say so, Gurnall sees this as devilish interference. He mentions also two critical points in Jesus' ministry: at his entrance into public ministry after his baptism, and at the end of his public ministry at the crucifixion, Jesus was subjected to the devil's ferocity. Gurnall warns Christians that the more public their place, the more eminent their service,

the more thou must look that the devil [will have] some more dangerous design or other against thee: and therefore if every private soldier needs armour against Satan's bullets of temptation, then the commanders and officers, who stand in front of the battle, much more. (I:73)

The Puritans also teach that the ordinances of worship, despite being given and commanded by God for the saints' duty and good, can become occasions of temptation. Watson writes that attendance upon the Word of God, prayer, or the sacrament is occasion for Satan to cast in his temptations. First, such fervour in a saint causes the devil fury; second, 'after we have had a full meal at an ordinance, we are apt to slumber and grow secure.'[30] Watson's observation dovetails closely with that of Owen and Gurnall, both of whom warn that genuine spiritual experience of God can, ironically, leave a saint dangerously open to seduction. (For the Puritans, most such experiences would be mediated through one or another of the activities they consider to be 'means of grace': reading of Scripture, prayer, godly discourse, attendance at Sabbath worship, preaching, the Lord's Table, and so on).

'After great manifestations of God's love, then the tempter comes' says Gurnall (I:74). Weeds of corruption sprout up even when the Christian is basking in the love of God. Favourable blessings from God can be seen by the saint as a sort of norm, and taken for granted; the Christian can become lazy, comfortable, and less than alert to the approach of the evil one. Gurnall uses the example of Peter who, having made his magnificent confession of the Messiahship of Jesus, and receiving Jesus' praise, immediately became the instrument of Satan in denying the necessity of Jesus' suffering (Matthew 16): 'so ambitious is Satan . . . to throw the saint into the mire when his coat is cleanest' (I:74). The devil takes advantage of Christians in the same manner as the

> cheater, who strikes in with some young heir, when he hath newly received his rents, and never leaves till he hath eased him of his money. (I:74)

John Owen's thought here is very similar to Gurnall's: he also observes that times of great spiritual enjoyment often become times of great danger, due to the 'malice of Satan and the weakness of our hearts'.[31]

Thus for some of the times and seasons during which, the Puritans warn, the saints are particularly vulnerable to the evil one.

VULNERABILITY OF SPECIFIC PERSONS

The Puritans insist that all Christians are engaged in spiritual warfare; they repudiate any idea that there are spectators and participants in this arena. All Christians, high and low, young and old, male and female, clergy and laity, are involved in this conflict. Yet they also teach that there are persons who, because of their particular role, office, position, or personal example, are in a special way important to the health of the family, church, or society. Such persons are therefore especially vulnerable to satanic attack.[32]

First, people who occupy positions of power and

influence are vulnerable. As Richard Baxter points out in his *Certainty of the Worlds of Spirits*, both Christ and Satan (as Christ's ape) make great use of human instruments,

especially of Princes and Pastors or Teachers, and Parents. These are the three great Organes (under Angels) appointed by God, ... Therefore it is the grand design of Devils to Corrupt these three, ... Asia, Africa, America and Europe, are doleful Monuments of the success of Devils, by making Princes, Priests and Parents their Instruments.[33]

Baxter says that, amazing as is the power of a witch, even more amazing is the evil the devils accomplish through 'Bishops, Priests and Princes, and Law-Makers.'[34]

William Gurnall concurs with his more famous Puritan contemporary. Gurnall invokes here the principle 'As the leader goes, so go the people', or to quote him, 'Corrupt the captain, and it is hard if he bring not off his troops with him' (I:79). He observes that in the political realm, sin at court can cost a kingdom (here again he may have had in mind the ignominious downfall of Charles I). The same obtains in the life of the Christian church. The New Testament is very specific in its call for holiness amongst church leaders; the whole church is likely to suffer severe damage if its leadership is corrupt. 'No such way to infect the whole town, as to poison the cistern at which they draw their water' (I:79).[35] How to confirm the unconverted in their lost condition? 'Let the preacher sew pillows under their elbows, and cry Peace, peace' (I:79). How to let the enemy succeed in bringing neglect and contempt upon the worship of God?

Let Hophni and Phinehas be but scandalous in their lives, and many both good and bad will 'abhor the sacrifice of the Lord.' (I:79; truly a word for today)

This emphasis surfaces repeatedly amongst the Puritans, and includes warnings to both ministers and the people they serve. Ministers have a fearful responsibility because people will follow them. Gouge says to his own brethren in the pulpit:

Let Ministers know that the precepts they give others, belong to themselves . . . Ministers are men as well as others; subject to like passions as others . . .[36]

In this matter the Puritans seem to place the most responsibility on the shoulders of leaders, exhorting them to watch how they live, lest they lead others astray. Yet they also strongly address the responsibility of all Christians to use critical discernment. John Downame actually warns against using leaders as personal examples, saying following should be by precept, not example. Since even the best leaders make many mistakes, following them in all particulars means 'we shall erre with them besides all our own errors.'[37]

Second, persons who are gifted with intelligence, and skill in the art of persuasion, are especially vulnerable to the devil (I:79). Thomas Brooks comments:

Satan hath his devices to ensnare and destroy the learned and the wise, . . . ; sometimes by drawing them to engage their parts and abilities . . . against the honour of Christ, . . .[38]

'Not many wise' are called, says the apostle (1 Corinthians 1:26), and Gurnall agrees. Satan is quick to utilize persons of intelligence, gifted with quick wits and a reasoning be the case; many of the Puritans are themselves first rank intellectuals, men of 'parts and policy' (I:79). Rather, the Puritans cultivate humility in regard to the intellect; they know mental acuity does not commend one to God, and that the intellect is not exempt from the effects of the Fall.

Intellectual prowess can be a marvellous tool for diabolical use: 'One great subtilty of the devil is to make use of such cunning, subtle-pated men'.[39] The more sophisticated and intellectually convincing an argument is, the better—especially if it is not true. 'Experts' often receive an adulation bordering on idolatry, playing into the devil's hands. Gurnall says:

A wicked cause needs a smooth orator; . . . As in particular, the instruments he useth to seduce and corrupt the minds of men are commonly subtle-pated men. (I:80)

He illustrates his contention from Scripture using the Pharisees, learned teachers of the day, who treated Christ with such contempt and hatred (I:80).

Thus the saints are urged to be very careful about giving their loyalty to apparently knowledgeable and gifted teachers. People are often led down the wrong path only because they are given enough truth to sound convincing:

Arius himself, and other dangerous instruments of Satan, were too wise to stuff their discourses with nothing but heterodox matter. (I:80)

Gurnall notes the elements that betray a false message clothed in truth and spoken by an attractive messenger: carnal reason, pride, and fleshly liberty. Even in pre-Enlightenment seventeenth-century England, Gurnall can say that carnal reason 'is the great idol, which the more intelligent part of the world worship' (I:81). He locates this as the root of the Arian and Socinian heresies. His stance, however, does not entail a rejection of reason. The Puritans believe strongly in natural law, and teach that reason can discern moral law, but not the Gospel: here reason must turn back 'or be content that faith should help reason over' (I:81). Thus rejection of the Gospel, or re-engineering it according to one's own ideas, is an elevation of reason over revelation. Carnal reason is a form of idolatry of the mind, and will betray the false teacher.

The next element betraying the false teacher is pride.

Man naturally would be a god to himself, . . . and whatever doctrine nourisheth a good opinion of man in his own eye, this is acceptable to him. (I:81)

The impressive thinker-speaker, as Satan's mouthpiece, will be a purveyor of teaching that exalts human goodness. Watson concurs: 'Satan encourages those doctrines that are flesh-pleasing. He knows the flesh loves to be gratified'.[40] The listening audience will tend to respond positively, since such ideas appeal to pride. While suscepti bility to pride is a generic condition—the diabolical 'sin of sins'—to which all human beings are subject, Thomas Brooks remarks that it is especially the educated and intelligent who fall prey to it. Satan has his devices for ensnaring and destroying such folk, encouraging them to be proud of their gifts, 'drawing them to rest upon their parts and abilities'.[41] 'Resting upon' entails trust; placing such trust in oneself is a form of self-worship.

The last element Gurnall names as identifying the false messenger is fleshly liberty. Satan will by such an instrument nourish the desire for freedom from restraint that characterizes fallen human nature. Churchmen who preach freedom from biblical morality often get a sympathetic hearing today; a similar situation obtained in Gurnall's day. Human beings resist wearing any yoke. If one must be worn, 'that will please best which hath the softest lining, and pincheth the flesh least' (I:81).[42]

Gurnall comments on the flak received by 'sincere teachers of the Word' (no doubt a reference to Puritans like himself) for pressing the issue of obedience to Scripture (I:81). Those who resist or downplay biblical norms are advocating a seventeenth-century version of 'cheap grace'; Gurnall says that 'they are content to afford heaven cheaper to their disciples, than Christ will to his' (I:82).

Third, persons with a holy reputation, those John Downame calls 'strong men in Christ', are vulnerable to the devil.[43] Gurnall observes that false prophets are not the only ones by whom people are led astray. He admits that truly holy people have been used by the devil to seduce others. Such is the frailty of the saints: Abram influences Sarai, so she lies for him (Genesis 12:10–20); the old prophet misleads the younger, who pays for his gullibility with his life (1 Kings 13:11). Gurnall and the other Puritans greatly emphasize the importance of living holy lives. They are also aware, however, of the danger that persons reputed to be saintly and holy will fail; and of how costly this is to the church.

Now as then, people look to persons of prominence for their cues in living, and often follow them. Gurnall warns those reputed to be spiritual exemplars:

O, how should this make you watchful, whose long travel and great progress in the ways of God, have gained you a name of eminency in the church, what you say, do, or hold, because you are file leading men, and others look more on you than their way! (I:82)

No doubt for Gurnall this statement is self-referential. He is well aware of the Puritan emphasis on the need for pastors to be both well prepared academically, and exemplary spiritually; they are to embody that which they preach (for the Puritans, it is not enough that the pastor be a facilitator, a sort of 'change agent' who can 'get the job done'). Gurnall here is the Puritan preacher, preaching to himself, as well as to his congregation.[44]

Fourth, the saints are vulnerable to attack through those to whom they are in close relationship. The devil often works through the relatives or friends of the person he wishes to destroy or disable. The Puritans have a fine sense of the agony of soul caused when this occurs; Gurnall observes that some 'martyrs have confessed' that their most difficult trial was overcoming the tears and prayers of their near and dear ones (I:82).[45] At the very beginning of *Pilgrim's Progress*, Bunyan illustrates this Puritan theme. Christian, his newly awakened conscience deeply troubled, warns his family of coming destruction and the need to escape. His family is filled with astonishment, not because they believe him but because it is apparent to them that

some frenzy distemper had got into his head: . . . when the morning was come, they would know how he did and he told them worse and worse. He also set to talking to them again, but they began to be hardened; they also sought to drive away his distemper by harsh and surly carriages to him: sometimes they would deride, sometimes they would chide, and sometimes they would quite neglect him: . . .[46]

When Christian flees the City of Destruction, his neighbours Obstinate and Pliable pursue him intending to restrain him by force if necessary. The friends and family depicted by Bunyan are not Christians at this point in the story. But the Puritans are keenly aware that hindrance comes to the saints not only from

our carnall friends, but also our spirituall kindred in Christ, who are of the same religion, and make the same profession with us.[47]

Bunyan again illustrates this very effectively later in his story, when Christian himself becomes the means of temptation and brings great trouble upon himself and his friend Hopeful. Wishing for a smoother path, they see By-Path Meadow, and a path running beside their way:

'Tis according to my wish, said Christian, here is the easiest going; come, good Hopeful, and let us go over.[48]

Thus Christian leads his friend, who follows him, and they both end up in the clutches of Giant Despair, locked in the dungeon of Doubting Castle.

These four examples of persons in and through whom the devils may work demonstrate the Puritan concern for both individuals and the community of faith. The devil chooses his instruments deliberately. He can use the unregenerate to mislead both Christians and non-Christians; and he can also use Christians themselves to do damage, both to themselves and to others.

The Puritans do not leave the saints in weakness; the next chapter examines the Christian armour and its use.

4

The Christian's Battlegear: Engaging the Enemy with Divine Resources

Warfare has many different characteristics; various types of warfare utilize different strategies for confronting the enemy. The Christian soldier, however, has only one basic position: stand (Ephesians 6:14). Gurnall exegetes this term as a military expression, an order used by officers to the soldiers under their command (I:275). Bayne describes what it means to 'stand':

A soldier standing orderly to fight, doth neither run forth to his peril, nor retire through cowardice, neither is beaten down by violence.[1]

Surrender or retreat in face of Satan's attacks is not a tactical tool for Christians; there is to be no yielding, only resolute resistance. The apostle Peter concurs with Paul: 'Whom resist steadfast in the faith' (1 Peter 5:9). This stance is to be maintained regardless of the cost. Gurnall says that such resistance may come to a point of shedding one's own blood (Hebrews 12:4), but for all that it 'alters not the case, nor gives a dispensation to shift for ourselves, by choosing to sin rather than to suffer' (I:276).

THE STANCE OF THE CHRISTIAN WARRIOR

The Christian has declared total war on sin and Satan; the nature of the warfare, considering the enemy, is unavoidable. The devil is not an enemy with whom one can negotiate:

> The soldier carries his prince's honour into the field with him, and so doth the Christian his God's, whenever he is called to contest with any temptation. (I:276)

The situation in spiritual warfare is not characterized by the ambiguities that obtain in human conflict, as when a war is clouded by unclear (or all too clear) motivation for evil or good, often on both sides. The Christian has no safety except in resistance. God and the devil are not busily negotiating in the background, setting up some 'mutually beneficial' settlement to end the conflict. The devil is the implacable foe of righteousness, and surrender means destruction. Christians, then, according to the Puritans, have no 'freedom of choice' in this matter: they must stand and fight.

The armour of the Christian is meant to defend the warrior in fight, not flight (I:277). This corresponds with the description Bunyan gives of his pilgrim's armour. Descending into the Valley of Humiliation, Christian, to his great distress, is confronted by the fiend Apollyon:

> Then did Christian begin to be afraid, and to cast in his mind whether to go back, or to stand his ground. But he considered again that he had no armour for his back, and therefore thought

that to turn the back to him might give him greater advantage with ease to pierce him with his darts; therefore he resolved to venture, and stand his ground.[2]

Retreat in the Puritans is seen as both a cowardly and disastrous strategy, for which God has provided no protection. They give several reasons why the devil is to be met only with resistance.

First, the devil is a coward (as has already been pointed out, this is a very common Puritan emphasis). He is like the school bully, apparently brave only because he picks on those smaller and weaker than himself. Satan, in actual fact, lives in terror, says Gurnall; as

a thief is afraid of every light he sees, or noise he hears, in the house he would rob; so Satan is discouraged where he finds the soul waking, and in any posture to oppose him. (I:278)

Therefore even the weakest Christian, with an active faith, is enough to put the devil to flight. Resistance is effective.

Second, the devil is persistent. Constant resistance is the only strategy Christians have, since if one area is defended but another neglected, Satan will be sure to enter at the weak point. If the saints yield in any sin, the evil one is there instantly to push them further than they ever intended to go.

Our best way, therefore, is to give him no hand-hold, not so much as to come near the door where sin dwells, lest we be hooked in. (I:278)

Third, the devil's persistence in the attack indicates the duration of the combat. It is permanent throughout this life; there is no time at which the Christian can say 'At last! I have finally arrived and can now relax.' There is no privileged ground in this life where the Christian can live as though the battle had ceased (I:114). Gouge says, in fact, that cessation of battle is an illusion, and a dangerous one (note again how complete Bunyan's Puritan vision is: his Enchanted Ground, where the pilgrims are nearly lulled to sleep, is one of the most dangerous areas of the entire journey).[3] If all is quiet, it is likely the devil has the upper hand.

Fierce combat doe give us more assurance that the Lord is still our God, and we his Souldiers, then light or no assaults: for if the Devill be our Lord, he can let us be quiet; but if our enemy, assuredly we shall feel his hand.[4]

Thus the Christian is to stand and resist from the beginning of spiritual life until the last breath. Gurnall emphasizes that this is an ever present condition; the warfare does not occur at only a few set battles, such as at conversion, or during affliction, or at the point of death (though the Puritans make much of these). Rather,

the enemy is ever in sight of us, yea, in fight with us. . . . from thy spiritual birth to thy natural death; from the hour when thou first didst set thy face to heaven, till thou shalt set thy foot in heaven. (I:114)

To this life, then, the Christian is called: a life of constant vigilance, of constant battle; a life filled with intrigue, attack and counter-attack, occasional defeats, but (by God's grace) increasingly frequent victories, assured that ultimate victory will be won.[5] To this end God has provided his people with appropriate weaponry, in order that they may successfully prevail in the fight.

THE ARMOUR

The 'whole armour of God' which the Christian is instructed to put on is not to be thought of mechanically.

It is not a 'thing' to do, a series of steps to take, a set of actions or rituals that, once completed, allow the Christian to say 'I am now clad in my armour.' The pieces of armour are figures describing a relationship with Christ. Gurnall can say the armour is Christ. He quotes the apostle Paul from Romans 13:14, 'Put on the Lord Jesus', 'where Christ is set forth under the notion of armour.' Gurnall points out that the apostle does not encourage Christians to put on various virtues as a philosopher might, but instead to put on Christ, implying that until Christ is put on, human beings are unarmed and defenceless (I:45).

It is not a man's morality and philosophical virtues that will repel a temptation, sent with a full charge from Satan's cannon, though possibly it may the pistol-shot of some lesser solicitation; so that he is the man in armour, that is in Christ. (I:45)

Thus the only armour (the 'complete armour') made available to Christians is Christ himself, and the graces of Christ. This all the Puritans teach; William Gouge says that to put on the armour is to put on

Christ himselfe: whereby is implied, that we should apply Christ unto ourselves: and so make use of him, and of all his actions and sufferings: yea also of all those graces, which he conveyeth unto us.[6]

To be without the armour of Christ leaves a person utterly exposed and vulnerable. Gurnall describes those outside of Christ very poignantly; their case is tragic and absolutely hopeless: 'A soul out of Christ is naked and destitute of all armour to defend him against sin and Satan' (I:45). Once a person comes to Christ, however, that soul is clad in armour. It remains to describe the various pieces of armour, and some of their function in spiritual combat.

THE BELT OF TRUTH

Paul says first of all, that Christians are to have their 'loins girt about with truth' (Ephesians 6:14). John Downame calls this piece of armour the 'girdle of veritie'. He describes it as

a broad studded belt used in wars in ancient times, wherewith the ioints of the breast-plate, and that armor which defended the belly, loines and thighes were covered.[7]

This belt served to secure the armour and hold it fast, and also to keep the soldier's body steady.[8]

The Puritans see in the belt of truth two aspects: 'sincerity to propound a right end, and knowledge of the word of truth to direct us in the right way to that end' (I:291). There must be sincerity—that is, honesty, truthfulness—of heart and life; and truth for the mind. The loins to be girded are the loins of the mind (as in 1 Peter 1:13). The loins, says Gurnall, are the centre of bodily strength, as the keel to the ship. Thus if the loins of the mind are not girded with truth and sincerity, the person will be a weak Christian indeed (I:292). As the warrior's belt is intended to stabilize him in battle, so the girding of the loins of the mind is intended to give the Christian stability: truth of doctrine for the mind, truth of heart for the will—to 'unite and establish both these faculties' (I:292).

Thus our minds and spirits need this girdle to strengthen them in every work we do, or else we shall act nothing vigorously. (I:292)

As the serpent often comes in the form of false teachers, it is important for Christians to have their minds secured with the belt of truth (I:293). Thus it is every Christian's obligation to labour for a sound grasp of the truth. Gurnall refers back to the Church Father Tertullian, who said of certain heretics in his own day, *persuadendo docent, non docendo persuadent*—'they teach by persuading, and do not by teaching persuade' (I:293). Thus error rarely tries to come in directly at the door of understanding, but will disguise itself appropriately to its target. Intellectual corruption is a present danger for the Christian, and thus a grasp of sound doctrine is critical in order not to be ensnared by an *erudita nequitia*, a learned kind of wickedness (I:295).

The belt of truth does not only protect against doctrinal error and deception, enabling the Christian to stand firm in the ancient faith. If the devil's assault on truth is not effective through deception, he will often employ force and intimidation. Thus the belt is necessary when Satan comes in the form of persecution. Gurnall illustrates this with yet another illustration drawn from the world of theatre:

> The bloodiest tragedies in the world have been acted on the stage of the church; and the most inhuman massacres and butcheries committed on the harmless sheep of Christ. . . . And as Luther said, Cain will kill Abel unto the end of the world. (I:304)

It is true that both ancient and modern persecutions against believers, particularly when they are social pariahs, excluded from access to political power, have a horrific history. When the church comes under persecution, as it periodically does, an 'established' grasp of the truth is not enough if it remains a purely notional, intellectual commitment. Bare opinion will not survive when it meets with severe pressure unless it is grounded in conviction and strength of resolution that does not back down.

Then a person becomes unconquerable, when from heaven he is endued with a holy boldness to draw forth the sword of the Spirit, and own the naked truth, by a free profession of it in the face of death and danger. (I:305)

THE BREASTPLATE OF RIGHTEOUSNESS

Ephesians 6:14 describes the second piece of armour 'commended to, and charged upon, all Christ's soldiers— a breastplate, and the metal it is to be made of, righteousness' (I:406).

Gurnall does not understand this to be the imputed righteousness of justification, which he assigns to the fourth piece of armour, the shield of faith (cf. Romans 4:11; I:407). Rather, he explains the breastplate as imparted righteousness, wrought by Christ within the Christian. Gurnall speaks for all the Puritans, who are unanimous on this point:

It is a supernatural principle of a new life planted in the heart of every child of God by the powerful operation of the Holy Spirit, whereby they endeavour to approve themselves to God and man, in performing what the word of God requires to be performed to both. (I:408)[9]

William Gouge well expresses the Puritan view as he explains why righteousness is compared to a breastplate. This piece of armour protects the vital organs of the body: heart, lungs, liver, and so on: 'the whole upper part of a mans body before, even from the neck to the thighs.'[10]

Thus, as long as breast and heart (the centre of one's being) are armed with righteousness—that is, a good conscience and a godly life—Satan's darts will not do mortal damage. The saints will receive wounds when, at times, the devil is successful in drawing them to some sin; 'but they are not wounded at the heart, because they do not sinne with full consent of will.'[11]

The breastplate of righteousness functions something like a bulletproof vest does today. A person can receive wounds in the extremities and yet live, but a wound in the vital organs, particularly the heart, usually means certain death (I:410). Sin is the weapon the devil uses to stab Christians in the soul; righteousness is the defence of the conscience against sin. Thus the person who means to truly be a Christian 'must endeavour to maintain the power of holiness and righteousness in his life and conversation' (I:412). This requires strenuous exertion in one's daily walk of faith; in such a manner walked the early Christians 'in whose veins,' saith Jerome, 'the blood of Christ was yet warm' (I:412).

This emphasis occurs repeatedly amongst the Puritans who address the subject. This righteousness does not entail sinless perfection, nor is it a Pharisaical 'works righteousness' focussing on external appearances. Its centre is an interior reality, the Spirit-wrought new heart, out of which pours the energy that results in visible godliness. The Puritan focus is on the bent of the heart and will, as when Paul Bayne says:

When the devil doth tempt us to sin, if the breast be covered with this purpose not to offend, then his suggestions will fall down like paper shot, and shall not pierce us.[12]

Bayne speaks of the heart's purpose; other Puritans speak of the same thing, using the language of active endeavour:

Their hearts are defended with the breast-plate of righteousness, that is, with an holie endevour and desire of serving God.[13]

There is a unique subtlety to this description of sanctifying righteousness, which helps explain why the Puritan movement is not a Pharisaical exercise in 'precisionism'. This seems to be what Jesus had in mind when he said in the Sermon on the Mount (Matthew 5:20):

For I say unto you, That except your righteousness shall exceed the righteousness of the scribes and Pharisees, ye shall in no case enter into the kingdom of heaven.

To beat the supreme legalists at their own game must seem impossible, unless one were to understand that righteousness does not consist simply in obeying a prescribed list of rules, but is a matter, first of all, of the heart. Puritan analysis of sin locates the problem at its centre in the human heart. The heart is the fountainhead, out of which flow evil deeds. In the same way, the active righteousness of the Christian is not first of all the good deeds, but the changed heart, which will then produce a working and active and lasting practical righteousness.

This new life in a Christian strains toward God. The saint is not a passive instrument, but is

active, and co-working with the Spirit in all actions of holiness; not as a lifeless instrument is in the hand of a musician, but as a living child in the hand of a father. (I:408)

This holiness galls the devil, whose greatest spite is against it: 'He can allow a man to have anything, or be anything, rather than be truly, powerfully, holy' (I:419). Gurnall feels the story of Job belongs precisely here. Satan's plundering of Job's estate, murdering his children, afflicting him with physical suffering, was all intended to cause Job to lose his breastplate of righteousness.

The lifeblood of holiness is that which this hellish murderer longs to suck out of the Christian's heart. (I:419)

Superstitious 'holiness', superficial, external 'holiness' does not bother the devil at all; in fact it is his work. The genuine article, however, draws him out. It is like the red flag to a bull. Real holiness of heart and life in a believer is intolerable to the devil; it is a statement of absolute defiance to its former master (I:420).

This again seems to be the point made by Bunyan when describing the fury of Apollyon against Christian, clothed now in righteousness and new armour. Christian says as much, in answer to Apollyon:

Apollyon, beware what you do, for I am in the King's highway, the way of holiness, therefore take heed to yourself.[14]

Knowing that Satan's fiercest opposition is to one's walk in holiness, the Christian is to walk directly into the teeth of the storm, as the pilgrim did. Then

shall not Satans darts pearce us, so long as we armed with a good conscience, and a godlie and innocent life . . . , the studie and holie endevour of a Christian to live in righteousnesse and true sanctification, doth so arme his mind, that Satan cannot wound the heart with any of his temptations.[15]

One of the great marks of the Puritans is what one might call their aesthetic of the Christian life, their sense of the beauty of holiness. The modern popular conception of Puritanism, as well as the modern use of the term generally, has been well captured in this verse:

> The Puritan through life's sweet garden goes
> To pluck the thorn, and cast away the rose;
> And hopes to please, by this peculiar whim,
> The God who fashioned it and gave it him.

The Puritans' response to such a caricature would be, 'Quite so, if you are looking at the Christian life through the devil's spectacles.' They had long since pointed out that the devil attempts to paint the holy life as one which hinders pleasure:

He labours to picture a holy righteous life with such an austere sour face, that the creature may be out of love with it. (I:456)

And he will simultaneously present the life of sin as one of pleasure rather than bondage.

The Puritans agree that the Christian life entails the denial of destructive 'pleasures', if so they can be called. The person pursuing such pleasures 'sucks dregs of wrath', as Gurnall puts it (I:459). The Puritans present a vision of holiness that is suffused with beauty and pleasure. People who have been touched by the grace of God are fitted to experience pleasures beyond any they had known, or could know: 'The fly finds no honey in the same flower from whence the bee goes laden away' (I:458). A holy life deepens and enhances legitimate pleasures immeasurably.

So a holy life not only protects the saints from lethal assault by the evil one; it also opens for them a world of pleasure which the devil can never counterfeit. This experience of blessedness and beauty is itself a kind of protection; those who have experienced the real thing can never after be deceived by the pretty poison the devil presents as though it were fine wine. Gurnall, depicting the pleasure of the life in Christ makes a powerful and remarkable statement here:

All is well. The coast is clear. He may say with David, 'I will lay me down in peace and sleep; for thou, Lord, only makest me dwell in safety,' Psalm 4:8. God will not—all but cannot—break his rest. As the unicorn heals the waters by dipping his horn in them, that all the beasts may drink without danger, so Christ hath healed creature-enjoyments, that there is no death now in the saints' cup. (I:459)

THE GOSPEL OF PEACE: THE CHRISTIAN SOLDIER'S FOOTGEAR

Describing the third piece of armour, Paul says Christians are to have their 'feet shod with the preparation of the gospel of peace' (Ephesians 6:15). Soldiers are in particular need of good footwear because of the rigours involved in war—long marches, rough terrain, bad weather.[16] Poor footwear exposes the soldier to injury and inhibits the success of the army in battle (I:559).

Calvin a century earlier says in a nutshell what all the Puritans understand this piece of armour to be:

He alludes, if I mistake not, to soldier's boots; for they were always reckoned among his armour, and were never in domestic use. The meaning is that as soldiers covered their legs and feet against cold and other injuries, so we must be shod with the Gospel, if we would pass unhurt through the world.[17]

For Gurnall, the foot is to the body what the will is to the soul: 'The foot carries the whole body, and the will the soul' (I:560). The man whose feet are well-shod is able to walk without fear where he likes. Thus the proper spiritual shoe prepares the will of the Christian to face any circumstance. Why is this shoe called 'the preparation of the gospel of peace'?

Because the gospel of peace is the great instrument by which God works the will and heart of man into this readiness and preparation to do or suffer what he calls to. (I:560)

Gurnall uses military imagery in depicting the Gospel as it calls and prepares believers to serve God. He pictures a captain, beating his drum in a city. The drumbeat is a signal that calls all those willing to voluntarily enlist for duty, to fight their prince's wars, and to be ready to go into the field and march at any time. In this way the Gospel calls men to the service of God, 'to stand ready for his service, whatever it costs them' (I:560).

The meaning of the Gospel of peace Gurnall expounds in its classic definition: the good news, joyful good news, that in Christ reconciliation has been wrought between sinners and God; men and women are restored to favour with their Maker and King (I:560, 561). Paul Bayne says the same: the sinner is given mercy, and along with mercy comes the realization that

everything that can befall is made for us: . . . Not life only, but death is ours; that is, is made to serve for our good. So the soul, knowing these things, is harnessed to go in the ways of tribulation.[18]

This good news ought to produce the greatest possible cheer available in this world. All people face tribulation, disappointment, and eventually death; the long range outlook is pretty gloomy. The gospel of peace changes all that, and the

Christian so shod is to be a happy individual, the church a joyful community. It is hard to reconcile the traditionally gloomy picture of the Puritans with what Gurnall says here:

To see a wicked man merry and jocund, or a Christian sad and dumpish, is alike uncomely. . . . I am sure God intended his people's joy in the feast of the gospel. . . . We do not commend his cheer, if it doth not cheer us. (I:489)

He cites the complaints of the world against melancholy and gloomy Christians, and upbraids those whose Christian experience denies the joy the Gospel declares. A Christian's joy, in fact, is one of the great attractions of the Gospel to the world. The Puritans insist that the manner of a Christian's walking displays the character of the Gospel he or she is proclaiming:

Give not them cause to think by your uncomfortable walking, that when they turn Christians, they must bid all joy farewell and resolve to spend their days in a house of mourning. (I:489)

Thus the Gospel, as seen by the Puritans, is not to issue in gloom, a sort of life-negating stoic resignation. Rather it prepares Christians to face any hardship, and infuses them with joy and good cheer that is not dependent on circumstance, but on the reality of restored fellowship with God.

The soldier's shoe determines the stance of the Christian in advance of whatever may come (thus is literally and metaphorically foundational), and prepares one to obey Paul's exhortation 'Stand therefore' (Ephesians 6:14). This is the stable foundation from which the saint can effectively fight.

THE SHIELD OF FAITH
The shield is the fourth piece of equipment mentioned by Paul: 'Above all, taking the shield of faith, whereby ye

shall be able to quench all the fiery darts of the wicked'
(Ephesians 6:16). Earlier it was noted that the Puritans
assign two different expressions of faith to different pieces
of armour: sanctifying faith to the breastplate of righteousness; justifying faith to the armour now under consid-
eration, the shield of faith. Justifying faith is

that act of the soul whereby it rests on Christ crucified for pardon and life, and that upon the warrant of the promise. (II:4)

This faith is not simply mental assent to truth, though it
includes that. It entails commitment, as Paul says in
2 Timothy 1:12: 'I know whom I have believed, and am
persuaded that he is able to keep that which I have com-
mitted unto him against that day.' Gurnall remarks that a
drowning man will not be saved by the sight of a man's
arm stretched out to him, but by seizing hold of it (II:6).

Faith's security is found in the promise of God to pardon those who trust in his Son, but—as Gurnall points
out—faith must observe the terms of the promise. He
remarks how many people make bold to come to God for
salvation,

but never think that the promise, which presents Christ to be
leaned on as a Saviour, presents him at the same time to be chosen
as a Lord and Prince! (II:7)

Justifying faith, then, is that act by which the whole person
trusts wholly upon the whole Christ for pardon from sin
and eternal life.

Thus Gurnall and all the Puritans define it. They know
no division amongst Christians in which some believe on
Jesus only as Saviour, and others opt also to take him as
Lord. The sinner is united to Christ as Lord and Saviour,

and it is this faith that is effective in quenching the enemy's fiery darts. This faith is recognized universally amongst the Puritans as chief of all Christian graces. Richard Sibbes speaks for all when he says:

Glorious things are spoken of the grace of graces [faith] in the Scriptures, God setting himself to honour that grace that yields up all the honour unto him in Christ: . . .[19]

Gurnall speaks in the same vein, placing faith even above love. On earth, he says, it is faith that is the conquering grace. As 1 John 5:4 has it, 'this is the victory that overcometh the world, even our faith' (II:12).[20]

Gurnall notes a double resemblance of the grace of faith to a shield. First, the shield defends the entire body; it is large enough, and can be moved to defend every part. Second, the shield is armour to the armour—it defends the other equipment of the soldier (II:8–10). Matthew Poole makes the same observation:

Faith, as receiving Christ and the benefits of redemption, is compared to a shield, . . . as being a sort of universal defence covering the whole man, and guarding even the other parts of our spiritual armour.[21]

Having defined the shield of faith, Gurnall demonstrates its usefulness when attacked by the fiery darts of enticements to sin. He uses the categories of temptation outlined in 1 John 2:16, 'the lust of the flesh, the lust of the eyes, and the pride of life.' These darts inflame the appetites of the body, lure the Christian into greed or covetousness, or set afire pride and ambition for worldly prestige and honour (II:78–82). Such temptations seem near to hand; they are immediately visible, tangible; the 'benefits' are immediate. Without faith, there is no defence against such things. Faith, however, is 'the substance of things hoped for, the evidence of things not seen' (Hebrews 11:1). By faith, spiritual reality (once a closed door) has come near:

It is the means by which there is present experience of realities which are future in time, or unseen as belonging to the spiritual sphere.[22]

Since faith enables the believer to live now in the future, and to experience spiritual things as realities even if not seen immediately, it provides a tremendous defence against those temptations which are immediately visible and temporal.

For example, the enticing dart of 'the lust of the flesh' inflames the appetites of the body while giving no true or lasting satisfaction (today such would be considered one of the many species of 'addictive behaviours'). Gurnall describes this condition accurately enough, as a kind of living hell, or 'hell above ground' for the enslaved creature (II:78). The shield of faith quenches this dart by stripping the temptation of its pleasing aspect, so the Christian can see through to its essence:

It gives him the native taste and relish of sin before the devil hath sophisticated it with his sugared sauce. . . . Faith hath a piercing eye. (II:79)

Faith not only reveals sin in its essence; it also shows the transient nature of those pleasures that accompany sin. Gurnall makes an interesting statement here: 'The pleasure of sin is extrinsical to its nature' (II:79). This is the Puritan affirmation of the goodness of the creation, and the goodness of pleasure as a part of creation. Sin, to mask its diabolical and deadly nature, is forced (hypocritically) to borrow from the good creation in order to provide a degree of temporary pleasure; a form of malevolent public relations. But this capital is soon spent; sin at last will be revealed to the sinner in all its falsity and bitterness. Faith sees all this beforehand, and thus repels the dart:

Now faith is a provident, wise grace, and makes the soul bethink itself how it may live in another world. (II:80)

The second fiery dart of enticement, the lust of the eyes, consists essentially of covetousness and greed: as the would-be adulterer looks lustfully upon the wife of another man, the covetous man lusts after his neighbour's wealth (II:80). Thomas Watson calls covetousness a 'mother sin, a radical vice . . . ; it is a plain breach of every one of the ten commandments.'[23] He and Gurnall agree that capitulation to this temptation is a failure of trust in the providence of God.[24] Faith repels this dart by persuading the Christian of God's fatherly provision. When the devil seeks to lure one into covetousness and grasping for advantage, faith enables the soul to say:

I am well provided for already, Satan; I need not thy pension; why should I play the thief for that which, if good, God hath promised to give? (II:81)

Faith delivers the soul from false security in depending on an abundance of things. God's blessing is the soul's safety: 'Faith is the cure of care.'[25] Faith knows this world is passing away; it sees the life that is to come, and lays up treasure in heaven, since all the baubles accumulated on earth will rust away. In Gurnall's picturesque language, faith discovers a world beyond the moon—and there lies faith's merchandise—leaving the colliers of this world to load themselves with clay and coals, while it trades for grace and glory. (II:81)

The third fiery dart of enticement is the pride of life, defined by Matthew Poole as

the ambitious affectation of the pomp and glory of the world, vain applause, the unmerited and overvalued praise of other men, . . .[26]

How is faith effective as a shield against the pride of life? Since pride fuels the temptation, faith cuts the supply. Pride lifts the soul up into the line of fire; faith humbles the Christian, and

a humble spirit loves a low seat; is not ambitious to stand high in the thoughts of others; and so, while he stoops in his own opinion of himself, the bullet flees over his head which hits the proud man on the breast. (II:83)

Rather than looking for the approbation of the world, for the praise and approval of one's contemporaries (besetting sin!), faith enables the saint to expect all his honour from Christ, of which source there is none higher (II:83). Brooks remarks:

True happiness is too big and too glorious a thing to be found in anything below that God that is a Christian's *summum bonum*.[27]

For the Puritans, faith is the supreme grace because it is the means by which human beings lay hold on God himself. Once that connection is established, the devil's offerings are poor fare indeed, and faith enables the Christian to see them as such.

THE HELMET OF SALVATION

In explaining the fifth piece of armour, the helmet of salvation (Ephesians 6:17), William Gurnall refers to another statement of Paul in 1 Thessalonians 5:8, 'And for an helmet, the hope of salvation.' The grace of hope is the helmet, and in this again the Puritans are in complete agreement (II:130).[28]

The Puritan exposition of hope has nothing to do with the idea of hope as uncertainty. Hope in modern usage is often a very doubtful thing; to have a 'hope so' attitude means one is hoping against hope! The Puritans use hope in rather the opposite way, as a robust expectation and certainty. John Downame says Christians do not turn from the fight

seeing by the Lord's assistance we doe assuredly hope for victory, and through his mercie and the merits of Christ doe expect . . . the garland of everlasting happiness.[29]

The same note is sounded wherever it is heard amongst the Puritans: hope is expectation, confidence, firm assurance. Gurnall gives his definition of hope as

a supernatural grace of God, whereby the believer, through Christ, expects and waits for all those good things of the promise, which at present he hath not received, or not fully. (II:130)[30]

This hope does not mean simply expectation of heaven at the end of warfare. John Downame, who emphasizes the garland to be won, and the 'palace of pleasure and never fading felicitie', nevertheless points out the present effectiveness of hope in the Christian's warfare:

For though Satan assault us . . . by offering unto us the riches, honours and pleasures of the world, . . . he shall not prevaile against us, if we be armed with this helmet of salvation.[31]

Bayne makes hope even more explicitly inclusive of temporal as well as ultimate deliverance and victory:

Not only hope of salvation, which shall be in the last day, but of all temporal deliverance from evil.[32]

All the Puritans agree regarding the utility of this piece of armour. A helmet in physical battle protects the warrior's head from bullet or sword; in the same way hope guards the soul (II:132). The helmet gives a soldier confidence because his head is protected; similarly, hope enables the saint to 'lift up his head' (Luke 21:28; II:133). As the Christian warfare is continuous and not sporadic, the helmet of hope is to be worn throughout life, until at the end God himself removes it to replace it with a crown of glory (II:134).

The helmet of hope is of use in resisting enslavement to past sins. Gurnall uses the analogy of the Israelites' bondage in Egypt, their submission and lack of any attempt to resist until brought hope of deliverance by Moses.

On a sudden their mettle returns, and their blood, that with anguish and despair had so long chilled, . . . grows warm again. (II:135)[33]

Like the enslaved Israelites, the soul without hope is powerless before sin; it is the devil's 'tame slave' (II:135). Hope of deliverance radically changes the situation. In the past, the soul has known no other master, nor the possibility of another. But with the glory of hope in Christ, the soul views past sins in a different light:

He presently vows the death of them all, and sets his hands at work how he may soonest and most effectually rid his hands of them. (II:136)

The Puritans point out another familiar area of temptation against which the helmet of hope is effective: materialism and worldly prestige. The perennial desire for wealth and popularity, then as now a trap promising contentment and happiness, delivering misery and poverty of soul. The Christian armed with hope (read: assurance) of riches in Christ recognizes the counterfeit nature of the world's offerings. No sane man will sell his

assured hope of the eternal kingdom of glorie, by yeelding himselfe the slave of sinne and Satan, to purchase for the present the worlds counterfaite shining excellencies . . .[34]

Hope expands the horizons of the Christian. The end-point of the Christian vision is located in eternity; worldly pursuits seen in that light are shown to be temporal and relative. People know, but are loath to admit, that this life and its treasure is passing away. Hope enables the Christian to admit this, because the best is yet to come. Thus is the believer freed from bondage to inordinate competition to 'get ahead', to 'be a success'.

As with each piece of the armour, skill in the exercise of Christian hope is a result of diligent effort. Victory in spiritual warfare is not mechanical; it does not happen automatically. In this we see the Puritans' dynamic understanding of the Christian life; it is not a matter of following certain steps, of just doing and saying the right things. The metaphors or symbols of armour are not static; they are qualities of the soul in relationship to Christ, relational realities. Thus they can, as the Puritans ceaselessly remind us, be improved upon; or they can be allowed to weaken and decay.

This is the case with the helmet of the hope of salvation.

Hope is not only a piece of armour to defend the Christian; it is also a target of the enemy, and itself needs defending. Note the initiative the Puritan expects his hearer to exercise:

Thy hope is the mark Satan's arrows are levelled at. . . . if at any time his dart reacheth it, and thy spirit begins to bleed of the wound . . . . Now labour, as for thy life, to hold up thy hope . . . and bow not by despairing to let the devil trample on thy soul. (II:176)

There is no passivity here. The soul is to rest completely in God's grace, and at the same time to engage all its powers to their fullest capacity. Both are true, and both are necessary, if hope is to be maintained.

THE SWORD OF THE SPIRIT, WHICH IS THE WORD OF GOD

Paul's sixth weapon of the Christian warfare is 'the sword of the Spirit, which is the word of God' (Ephesians 6:17).

The centrality of biblical authority to the Puritans is so well known it hardly needs to be restated. M. M. Knappen notes the importance to all human social movements of some foundational principle:

In Puritanism this ultimate principle was the doctrine of the unique and complete authority of the Bible. . . . The reason for this absolute and universal supremacy was the divine nature of the Bible. It was not only the pure word of God but the 'Scripture of God,' the writing of the Most High.[35]

The very format of the Westminster Confession demonstrates the accuracy of Knappen's statement: the first chapter is entitled 'Of the Holy Scripture'.[36]

All the Puritans hold 'the sword of the Spirit' to be the

Bible. Thomas Watson, in his exposition of the Shorter Catechism, says of the Scripture 'This sword of the Spirit cuts down vice.'[37] Gurnall makes the same explicit 'this is that' connection between the Bible and the sword (II:194).

Paul Bayne's comment is helpful here. He writes that the 'word of God' in Ephesians 6:17

is, whatsoever out of the written word we have by reading and hearing, or what God doth teach us by experience, agreeable with that which is in the word written.[38]

In this statement, Bayne shows that what is important is the content of Scripture. The Bible is not a 'sacred object', to be superstitiously regarded as magically effective. Rather, the content of the message of the Bible is to be appropriated and applied by the believer.

The Puritans insist that the Word of God is inseparable from its source and ultimate author; thus it is called the sword of the Spirit. Gurnall says that the Ephesian passage does not simply say 'take the spiritual sword', but refers to the Holy Spirit personally: and the Spirit is the author of Scripture. 'A weapon it is which his hand alone formed and fashioned; it came not out of any creature's forge' (II:219).

Owen's 'Reason of Faith' is an important Puritan statement regarding the relationship of Spirit and Scripture, affirming both the Spirit's authorship of Scripture, and the necessity of his work to illuminate the mind to believe that this is so (thus rendering the sword usable to the Christian).[39]

The Puritans are not deists regarding the work of God in creation, and they are not deistic in their conception of the Bible: it is not simply the 'rule book' or the 'owner's manual'. The Word of God is an objective, written reality; but the Spirit who gave it in the past is the one who speaks it still in the present. He is the interpreter, as Gurnall says:

The Scriptures must be read, and can be understood, by that Spirit alone by whom they were made. (II:219)

And only the Spirit of God can make the Word of God efficacious and powerful; he it is who causes the inspired written word to inspire the heart of the child of God. The Holy Spirit

lays his weight on the truths we read and hear, to apply them close, and as it were cut their very image in our minds and hearts, . . . Not all our study and inquiry can fix the mind, or pacify the heart in the belief of the word, till the Spirit of God comes. (II:220)[40]

Thus the Puritans agree: the sword of the Spirit is the Word of God, the Scriptures, authored, given, and empowered by the Holy Spirit. But why is the Word of God described as a sword? Here again Puritan unity of perspective is displayed. Perhaps they take their cue (as often is the case) from Calvin, whose statement in his Ephesian commentary the Puritans both concur with and amplify:

If the Word of God shall be efficacious in us through faith, we shall be more than sufficiently armed both for repelling and for putting to flight the enemy.[41]

Calvin characterizes the sword as both defensive and offensive, and the Puritans repeat this formula throughout their writings. Early on, William Perkins points out that Christ parried Satan's tempting suggestions by quoting the written word. Rather than overthrowing the tempter by his power as the Eternal Son, or calling on legions of angels, Jesus had recourse to Scripture. This he did, says Perkins, especially for the instruction of those who believe, so they may know that the Word of God is the supreme weapon for routing Satan;

hence Paul calleth it the sword of the spirit, because it serves not onely for our defence, but also to wound Satan, and to put him to flight.[42]

Gurnall half a century later repeats this description. He comments that the sword, as it is the weapon of general and constant use to soldiers, used both for defence and offence,

it most fitly sets forth the necessity and excellent use of the word of God, by which the Christian both defends himself, and offends, yea cuts down before him all his enemies. (II:219)

Here again, John Bunyan has distilled this Puritan theme and given it picture form, particularly in regard to the sword as an offensive weapon. When the pilgrim (newly armed) descends into the Valley of Humiliation, he meets his former master Apollyon. Unable to persuade Christian to re-enter his service, Apollyon attacks him ferociously. Christian defends himself with sword and shield the best he can. Badly wounded, he gives ground, and is eventually thrown down, dropping his sword. Apollyon moves in for the kill; but at that moment

Christian nimbly reached out his hand for his sword, and caught it, saying 'Rejoice not against me, O mine enemy! when I fall I shall arise,' and with that gave him a deadly thrust, which made him give back as one that had received his mortal wound: Christian perceiving that, made at him again, saying, 'Nay, in all these things we are more than conquerors through him that loved us.'

And with that Apollyon spread forth his dragon's wings, and sped him away, that Christian saw him no more.[43]

The critical importance of this weapon gives rise amongst the Puritans to some of their more pointed criticisms of the papacy. Here they show their pedigree as faithful children of the Reformation. Speaking of the Roman Church's denial of the Scripture to the common people, Calvin had said

And those who take from a Christian people the Word of God, do they not despoil them of their necessary armour, so that they perish without a struggle?[44]

Keith Thomas relates the view of the Protestant reformers toward the ritual of the Roman Catholic Church: they

rejected the magical powers and supernatural sanctions which had been so plentifully invoked by the medieval Church.... But it was not the rediscovery of classical magic which underlay the complaints of the reformers: it was the basic ritual of the Catholic Church.[45]

This perspective forms the crux of the Puritan complaint (after Calvin), critiquing Roman ritual as a worthless substitute for the Word of God. The denial of the Scripture to the people is a 'damnable practise', says William Perkins of the Roman Catholic Church of his day,

who locke up the word of God from their people in an unknown tongue, and commend unto them for their defence against spirituall enemies other devices of their owne, as holy water, crossing, crosses, etc. which they highly commend as meanes of speciall strength and force to vanquish the Divell; when as indeed the word of God is the onely true and trustie weapon, whereof while they deprive their people, they send them forth naked and unarmed to encounter with Satan.[46]

Shortly after Perkins, Downame says the same thing in his *Christian Warfare*, speaking of the wickedness of those who take the weapon away from the people of God, reserving it for the clergy and betraying the people into Satan's power.[47]

A half century later, and William Gurnall says substantially the same thing with great force. As noted before, Gurnall's references to the papacy are quite rare. In this instance, however, he does speak, and with all the vigour Puritans are noted for. He charges Rome with cruelty to the souls of people in denying them the only weapon with which they can defend themselves:

This we may well wonder at, that men who know the Scriptures—as many of their leaders do—and acknowledge their divinity, dare be so impudent and audacious [as] to intercept this letter sent from the great God to the sons of men. (II:231, 232)

This universal criticism of Rome's handling of the Bible at that time throws into bold relief two great facts about Puritan spirituality (these have received occasional mention already in this book). First, it is dynamic, not static; personal, not mechanical/magical—thus the critique of Roman ritual as worthless (or worse, positively harmful) magic or superstition. The Puritans reprobate any view of spirituality that suggests any sort of automatic efficacy. They oppose this in Rome, and they oppose it in their own practice as well. Thus they insist that the denial of the Bible to people is the worst sort of crime, disarming people of the truth which is their defence and weapon, only to replace it with incantations and talismans.

Second, Puritan spirituality is seen to be all-inclusive and egalitarian; it encompasses the whole people of God, with no exceptions, and no special classes. Thus the Bible is given by God 'not to any party or sort of men, but to every man where it comes' (II:232). Gurnall says that Paul's instruction is meant for everyone. Every saint is to be clad with the armour of God,

So that to whom he directs the former pieces, to these he gives the sword of the word to use. Now those you shall find are persons of all ranks and relations; husbands and wives, parents and children, masters and servants. He would have none be without this sword. (II:197)

All Christians, to the best of their ability, are to engage themselves fully in the study of the Word of God, equipping their minds and spirits to quit themselves well in their part of the battle.[48]

This aspect of Puritan teaching—the necessary engagement of every person in the study and use of the Word of God—leads to a final point. The Puritans repeatedly tell us that the Bible is not only to be used to rout the devil; the sword is to be used for self-surgery. It is the instrument of death to indwelling sin. Henry's commentary shows this use of the sword. Scripture

being hid in the heart will preserve from sin . . . and will mortify and kill those lusts and corruptions that are latent there.[49]

The end to which the use of the sword is directed is the perfecting of each soul; the hewing down and destruction of indwelling sin is not a purely negative work. It is the work of the Holy Spirit in clearing the way for the growth of the new creature; as William Gurnall says:

This is not a book to be read by the lowest form in Christ's school only, but beseeming the highest scholar that seems most fit for a remove to heaven's academy. It is not only of use to make a Christian by conversion, but to make him perfect also. (II:196)

PRAYER: PUTTING ON THE ARMOUR

Following his exhortation to put on the whole armour of God, the apostle Paul concludes: 'Praying always with all prayer and supplication in the Spirit, and watching there-unto with all perseverance and supplication for all saints' (Ephesians 6:18).

The Puritans place an enormous emphasis upon the importance of prayer, more perhaps than on any other single activity of the Christian life. William Gurnall, for instance, devotes several hundred pages to expounding the six pieces of armour. It is significant that his exposition of prayer, following the armour, is far longer than his comments on any single piece; it constitutes approximately one-quarter of the entire book. For Gurnall, it is not so much another piece of the armour, as it is the context in which the armour is to be used. The spiritual armour will only be effective so long as it is treated with the oil of prayer (II:288). Gurnall says 'what the key is to the watch, that [is] prayer to our graces—it winds them up and sets them agoing' (II:288).

Other Puritans also point out the crucial linkage between prayer and the armour. William Gouge, writing of Christian weakness, says:

Now because of our selves, we are as children, and no better able to wield this Armour of God, then David the Armour of Saul, the apostle addeth that heavenly exercise of praier, . . . [50]

Gurnall shows the need for the armour to be maintained by prayer, Gouge the necessity of prayer in the use of the armour. John Downame says prayer is necessary even to put the armour on in the first place. The armour is God's gift, 'the graces of God's Spirit'. God sends the Holy Spirit in response to prayer (Luke 11:13):

And he commeth not alone, but bringeth with him our spirituall armour, even all his graces fit for to arme us in the spirituall combat . . .[51]

Another writer says in a similar vein, 'Prayer must buckle on all the other parts of our Christian armour.'[52]

The Puritans are prayer-oriented Christians; that is, they are God-oriented. They recognize that their learning, their attendance upon divine duties, even diligent attention to Scripture, counts for nothing if they do not genuinely enter into the presence of God. Gurnall says as much. He tells his listeners, after he has described the Christian outfitted in armour, that the soldier lacks nothing now but 'the presence of his general' (II:288). Without the living presence of God, a Christian in armour is 'all dressed up with no place to go.'

As every Christian is a warrior, the work of prayer in order to be properly armed is to be engaged in by everyone. Here the Puritan trademark is seen again: Christian soldiery is for everyone, not for an élite 'corps'. John Owen says of prayer 'the use of it is here enjoined unto all believers, none excepted, men and women'.[53] And prayer is not to be engaged in lethargically, or haphazardly: prayer demands engagement, exertion, attention. Since the devil will use the saints' laziness to insinuate himself into their lives, Christians are to take the initiative. They are to talk to themselves, stir themselves up, confess their sins, and

these holy affections will prevent the soul's wandering disposition, so also make it more difficult for Satan to throw in his injections. (II:324)

The saints are to cultivate an attitude of prayer at all times: 'endeavouring to keep our hearts in a praying frame'.[54] This is to be a settled disposition. Prayer is the subtext of every waking moment, every duty, every activity. The Christian (as the old song has it) is to be 'ready, willing, and able' to pray at any and every opportunity.

At the same time, despite the Puritans' serious call to Christians to set their hearts in a praying frame, they recognize that this is impossible unless the Holy Spirit gives the gift of prayer to the saints. They are emphatic that 'Prayer is the creature's act, but the Spirit's gift':

Christ is the door that opens into God's presence, and lets the soul into his very bosom; faith is the key that unlocks the door; but the Spirit is he that both makes this key, and helps the Christian to turn it in prayer, so as to get any access to God. (II:486)

Paul Bayne makes the same point. Regarding Paul's exhortation to the Ephesians to pray 'in the Spirit', Bayne says it signifies

the fountain whence it must spring, from our spirits, moved by the Spirit of God, which is the inditer of prayer.[55]

Along with reminding the saints of their duty to pray, and showing that this duty can only be performed in the power of the Holy Spirit, the Puritans provide a rich body of teaching on the actual practice of prayer. The first thing to note is that prayer to the Puritans is nearly always a vocal event; prayer is, on most occasions, spoken aloud. John Owen, in his *Discourse of the Work of the Holy Spirit in Prayer*, opposes contemplative prayer in which there is supposed to be complete cessation of thought or speech. He refers to the example of Jesus himself, who both prayed in words, aloud, and taught his disciples the same, showing the 'necessity and usefulness of vocal prayer.'[56] Owen in fact considers that vocal prayer, led by the Holy Spirit, leads the mind, which in turn gives rise to further expression. Thus the mind is disciplined to adhere to prayer, rather than to wander, since the wandering, meandering mind becomes open to demonic suggestions. Owen seems here to speak of his own experience in prayer:

And we have experience that an obedient, sanctified persistency in the use of gracious words in prayer hath prevailed against violent temptations and injections of Satan, which the mind in its silent contemplations was not able to grapple with.[57]

Regarding the content of Christian prayer, the Puritans are generally in agreement. Sometimes they use slightly different categories, but these often overlap and cover essentially the same ground. Paul Bayne, for example, basing his comment on 1 Timothy 2:1, categorizes Christian prayer like this:

First, Deprecative, or prayers that ask removal of evils; 2. Petitions, or wishes, of good things; 3. Intercession for others; 4. Thanksgiving.[58]

Gurnall divides prayer into two general categories: request, or petitionary prayer; and thanksgiving.

These two are like the double motion of the lungs, by which they suck in and breathe out the air again. In the petitionary part of prayer we desire something at God's hands; in thanksgiving we return praise to him for mercies received from him. (II:425)

Under petitionary prayer, Gurnall makes three further divisions, which actually match closely with Bayne's.

First, precatory prayer, in which Christians ask some good thing from God, through Christ (II:426).

Second, deprecatory prayer,

wherein we desire of God, in the name of Christ, the removal of some evil felt or feared, inflicted or threatened. (II:431)

Deprecatory prayer is useful in spiritual conflict, since it deals with one's own sin and guilt. It is also to be used in the midst of suffering as another aspect of warfare praying, since Satan often attacks saints who are undergoing affliction: 'Deprecate the snare and temptation that suffering may expose thee to' (II:440).

Third, imprecatory prayer is another eminently useful kind of prayer in battle 'wherein the Christian imprecates the vengeance of God upon the enemies of God and his people' (II:444). Gurnall warns Christians here to take care not to imprecate one's personal enemies, and to pray against plots, not persons (II:445).

Along with giving detailed instruction regarding the content of prayer, the Puritans speak of situational prayer; that is, the various occasions when prayer is to be offered. While cultivating an attitude of prayer at all times, the Puritans are also very matter of fact about the demands of life. They are earthy Christians; they do not advocate a sort of super-spirituality which denies the importance of the so-called 'mundane' aspects of life. Thus they say prayer is not to overthrow other legitimate duties.[59] Yet there are to be definite times where prayer is the main business: 'we should keep up constant times of prayer, and be constant to them.'[60]

There are to be times when prayer has a social character. One aspect of social prayer is the private devotional time of a family together, of which the Puritans make much (II:378). The family is like a little church, and devotion (or lack thereof) in the home spells success or failure for the public church, and for the society at large.

The public aspect of social prayer is in the gathered church at worship (II:391). Gurnall draws attention to the strength there is in a group, and the need for a unified church to approach God together:

How influential then must church communion needs be . . . when they shall consider they go to the same public school of the ministry, sit at the same table of the sacrament, suck the same breasts of ordinances, and lie together in the bosom, yea womb, of the same church. (II:394)

Such communion in prayer is necessary for defence against the church's enemies:

Such an army are the saints when they stand in communion together. . . . the soldier [is] safe when marching with the army, but snapped when he straggles from it. (II:394)

While they emphasize the need for social prayer, the real eloquence of the Puritans seems reserved for the value and need of secret prayer. Here, too, there are several forms of prayer. There is a kind of secret prayer that is regular and ongoing, a consistent time of meeting with God (such as Jesus practised, Luke 22:39). The character of such prayer is absolute privacy, and absolute candour. It is not to be advertised; it is communion between the soul and God alone. Gurnall is very blunt: 'Strip thy soul naked, and shuffle not with God' (II:377). The saint, while maintaining reverence before the Lord, is to be free and absolutely open.

Another type of secret prayer is what the Puritans call 'ejaculatory prayer'; such prayer can be offered anywhere and anytime. Henry's *Commentary* advocates mixing ejaculatory prayer with everyday business, speaking quietly to God amidst the common tasks of 'ordinary' people.[61] Gurnall defines such prayer as

the lifting up of the soul to God upon a sudden emerged occasion, with some short but lively expression of our desires to him. (II:363)

Sometimes prayers of this type may be vocal, sometimes not; such 'arrow' or 'dart' prayers may be shot into heaven 'without using the tongue's bow' (II:363). These dart prayers are effective in destroying thoughts which the devil tries to inject into the mind. If the saint cannot pull out the long sword of solemn prayer, says Gurnall, use this dagger (II:365).

Ejaculatory prayer may be a response to distress, but deep crisis gives occasion for what Gurnall calls 'extraordinary prayer'. Ordinary prayer, both social and secret, is food. Extraordinary prayer is physic (II:402): such medicine is not in constant use; it is to be used especially in times of difficulty, confusion about the truth, affliction, or temptation (II:406–408). In this connection Owen seems to qualify his strong advocacy of rational, vocal prayer. He recognizes extremities in the saints' lives:

There may be such interpositions of temptations and desertions as that the soul, being overwhelmed with them, may for the present be able only to 'mourn as a dove,' or to 'chatter as a crane,'— that is, not to express the sense of their minds clearly and distinctly, but only as it were to mourn and groan before the Lord in brokenness of spirit and expressions. But this also is sufficient for their acceptance in that condition.[62]

Extraordinary prayer is a response to extraordinary circumstances, as when faced with devils that only come out by prayer and fasting (Matthew 17:21; II:408). Gurnall speaks of times when saints are buffeted by the devil, or beset by some internal corruption, and

can not, with the use of ordinary means, quench the one or master and mortify the other. If the short dagger of ordinary prayer will not reach the heart of a lust, then it is time to draw out this long sword of extraordinary prayer upon it. (II:408)

The Puritans thus place before us a compelling vision of the life of prayer, accessible not just to those who can devote large amounts of time to spiritual exercises, but to every Christian in every sort of circumstance. And it is through prayer—not as a ritual to be performed, but as a relationship with the living God—that Christians are armed for the conflict, and kept in the midst of their warfare. The saints of the past are to be our examples:

The great spoils which they ever got from their enemies was in the field of prayer. If Moses send Joshua into the valley against Amalek, himself will be on the mount to storm heaven by his prayer, while he is engaged in fight with the enemy below, and the victory it is plain was not got by Joshua's sword, so much as Moses' prayer. (II:290)

Prayer is actually the battle stance of the believer. Ironically, for the Puritans, in order to stand most firmly in the battle, the saints must be upon their knees.

5

Conclusion

We have investigated the mainstream Puritan view of spiritual warfare as represented by some of its leading proponents, especially William Gurnall. The Puritan portrait of the enemy has been displayed: that enemy is not one, but many. These are wicked spiritual beings, the devils; unbodied intelligences, created good but corrupted by rebellion against their Creator.

The devils—and Satan, their prince—possess rule and power over the human race, allowed because of humanity's own rebellion. Their power over the wicked is an aspect of the judgment of God; their harassment of the saints, under the sovereign hand of God, serves to build up God's people, and to undo the devils' work even as they perform it.

The primary rule of the devils is over the wicked, who serve them religiously, often unaware of it. However, those against whom the devils' greatest ferocity is directed are the children of God. Real spiritual battle only takes place between the saints (who by their new birth have become children and friends of God), and their evil former masters. The devils, enraged by their lost sovereignty and jealous of the saints' favoured position, seek to strike Christians, and through them, God.

We have looked at the Puritan picture of the embattled saints, regenerated human beings in whom the love of self and Satan has been replaced by the love of God. The devils seek to pinpoint remaining sin and weakness in the saints, choosing carefully times and circumstances when the saints are most vulnerable. They also seek especially to tempt human beings who occupy pivotal and important roles and positions, so as to hurt both them and those who are influenced by them. This led us on to the display of the battlegear available to Christian soldiers, as listed by the apostle in Ephesians 6. The armour was seen to be Christ himself, and the gifts and graces he imparts to believers, appropriated and applied to the heart and life.

The pieces of armour are the belt of truth, sincerity and truth of heart and mind; the breastplate of righteousness, explained by the Puritans to be a life of sincerity and godly obedience; the soldier's footgear, which is the secure footing provided by the Gospel; the shield of faith, that is, justifying faith, the most important piece of armour and that which guards all else; the helmet of salvation, which is the grace of hope, that is, certainty of victory in Christ; and the sword of the Spirit, the truth of Scripture, applied to the believer by the Holy Spirit, and given as the only offensive weapon to drive Satan away, as Christ did in the wilderness.

The armour being metaphorical for the graces of Christ, it is put on by means of believing prayer. Prayer also maintains the armour, and enables the believer to use the armour effectively.

Having recapitulated the major points, there remain

several prominent characteristics of Puritan thought and practice to be highlighted.

PURITAN UNITY

This study demonstrates that the Puritans constitute a formidable school of thought in their understanding of spiritual warfare: both in their acceptance of its reality, and the response they offer to it.

It is impossible to account for this unity by simply seeing the Puritans as another 'in-group'. The Puritans are highly educated men, most of them steeped in classics and ancient languages, intelligent and cultured individuals; Christian humanists. Their theological and spiritual unity is largely a result of their immense (and intense) devotion to Scripture, and their conviction that it is the living voice of God.

The Reformation emphasized the primacy of Scripture and its exposition, exemplified supremely in the commentaries on Scripture produced by John Calvin. The Puritans took over this emphasis with great seriousness, and devoted themselves to biblical learning and application. William Haller makes the point very well:

Actually, the preachers, Calvinist though they were in varying degrees, referred as often to St. Augustine as to the author of the Institutes, but were chary on principle of citing any merely human authorities whatsoever. ... Calvin's most important effect upon the preachers was to send them posting back to Scripture, particularly to the epistles of Paul, to Paul's life in Acts, and so to the gospels and to the rest of holy writ. Consequently there is less of the manner and spirit of Calvin in the preachers' lives and writings than of the apostle to the Gentiles.[1]

It matters not which Puritan one reads; each writer is absolutely saturated in Scripture, both Old and New Testaments. Each demonstrates a remarkable grasp of the entire canon, citing almost at will from any place at all, often from sections of Scripture (like the Minor Prophets) which are almost unknown territory to many modern Christians.

The Puritans provide an example of the unity possible when Christians seriously and unequivocally submit their minds and lives to the authority of Scripture as the voice of God, allowing it to shape their thinking and their living.

PURITANS AND REGENERATION: THE NEW CREATURE

At first glance, particularly in a book on spiritual warfare which details some of the weaknesses of Christians, the strength of the Puritan doctrine of regeneration may not be obvious. But it should be noted, because regeneration largely explains why there is any battle—and consciousness of that battle—at all.

The Puritan depiction of the sin-enslaved creature is that of an ignorant soul not aware of its own ignorance, a bound soul not aware of its own captivity, an enslaved soul not aware of its own slavery, a damned soul not aware of its ultimate destination. The Puritans call the sinner Satan's 'tame slave'.

Regeneration changes this whole dismal picture. The principle of new life has been planted within the human heart by the Holy Spirit. The believer is a new creature. Such a soul is now awake, not asleep; aware of its former enslavement; and alive to the reality and identity of its former master. Suddenly there is consciousness of battle! The remnants of sin in the believer make their malignant presence felt; Satan comes to 'blow up the coals' of remaining corruption.

The regenerated person thus, in some ways, has precipitated the battle. The saint is an insurgent in Satan's territory, and becomes a target. The Christian is now an active agent, rather than a passive slave. And armed with the weaponry provided by God, the saint becomes a threat to Satan's kingdom.

Such is the Puritan view. The strength of the Puritan doctrine of regeneration leads to the next point.

THE RIGOUR OF PURITAN DISCIPLESHIP

The Puritans' view of regeneration explains the stringency of their demand (really a New Testament demand) for discipleship from every believer.

Despite the seriousness with which the Puritans treat Satan and indwelling sin, their emphasis is far more centred on God and his glory and power, the glory of Christ, and the work of the Holy Spirit in the believer. The new creature is drawn into the life of the Trinity; is called to engage with vigour the new life; is to draw near to God and live with fortitude, obedience and faithfulness in the sinful world.

This is the vision of the Puritans, and this is why they can call each saint to do battle without fear and with all their strength. If you are a new creature in Christ, they say, that new life will manifest itself in vigorous action toward God, and against sin and Satan. The very nature of the new life implanted in the soul is that it strains toward God; the saints' responsibility is to nurture and encourage that life, help it to grow, weed out and kill everything that can harm or hinder it.

Thus each person is called to be active, to put on the

spiritual armour that protects this inner life, and do battle in the grace of Christ against the malice of Satan.

THE RELATIONAL CHARACTER OF THE PURITAN LIFE

Closely related to the last point is the fact that the Puritan life is not a life where spiritual success is attained through ritual, spiritual mechanics, or magic. It is relational, not technological. It is a life lived in fellowship with God, with others, and with oneself.

Success in the spiritual warfare is characterized by this relational emphasis as well. The Christian's armour is not to be seen as a sort of superior spiritual technology, but rather the arming of the soul in relation to Christ, as Christ imparts his grace to that soul. This is an important emphasis, particularly in this day, when people often want quick solutions to problems. The Puritans remind us that only living in friendship and obedience to God is there true human growth, and healing of 'dysfunctional' aspects of human life.

PURITAN OPTIMISM: HOPEFULNESS

Ironically, the Puritans show us that it is a hopeful stance—in fact, the only hopeful stance—to admit human evil and limitation, and the existence of the devil. To the Puritans, the denial of these is both idiotic and disastrous. To deny the reality of personal evil is a 'fond conceit'. They are very matter of fact about this. To deny sin and the devil is to deny what is: it will not make these realities go away. Such denial is simply the ostrich response of putting one's head in the sand (or under the covers) in hopes that unpleasant realities will go away.

The Puritans take the existence of devils seriously. Their

concern is similar to the concern a father should have if he learns that his neighbour is a child molester. Denial would hardly be a wise response; and it certainly would not protect one's children.

The Puritans tell us, wake up! Stop being surprised at the disastrous moral/spiritual failure and lunacy that exists on all sides. Sin is real; the devils exist, they are powerful, and they want your soul. Sociological analysis, educational reform, and whatever other human solutions are put forward, will never address the fundamental issue. The poison that exists in the fallen universe has only one effective antidote.

Only in such 'pessimism' is there hope. Denial is a solution of despair, as it is simply an escape into fantasy; the evil remains, and will destroy any illusion eventually.

Recognition of the existence of evil, if it offers the wrong antidote—or none—is as ineffective as denial. The Puritans show us the way to face evil, and participate in overcoming it in ourselves and in the world, through the grace that is in Christ Jesus.

The Puritan teaching and practice of spiritual warfare is an enduring legacy, and is of great value in our own day. Many Christians are again confronting the reality and necessity of spiritual warfare; the Puritans will prove to be good and reliable guides in the battle.

Notes

Chapter 1   Introduction

1. See, for example, a cross-cultural survey of this phenomenon in Jeffrey Burton Russell, *The Devil: Perceptions of Evil from Antiquity to Primitive Christianity* (Ithaca, New York: Cornell University Press, 1977).

2. Joe Fisher, *Hungry Ghosts: An Investigation into Channeling and the Spirit World* (Toronto: Doubleday Canada Limited, 1990). Fisher borrows his title from a Tibetan Buddhist term. 'Hungry ghosts' refers to individuals who, at physical death, are still entangled in desire. Thus trapped they are thought to remain on the 'lower planes', lurking about living, enfleshed human beings; see p. 255.

3. William Perkins, *A Discourse of the Damned Art of Witchcraft* (Cambridge: Thomas Pickering, 1610).

4. Richard Baxter, *The Certainty of the Worlds of Spirits* (London: T. Parkhurst and I. Salusbury, 1691).

5. Cotton Mather, *The Wonders of the Invisible World* (London: John Dunton at the Raven in the Poultry, 1693. Repr., London: John Russell Smith, 1862).

6. See Carl Raschke's recent book *Painted Black* (San Francisco: Harper and Row, 1990).

7. William Gurnall, *The Christian in Complete Armour: A Treatise of the Saints' War Against the Devil*, with a Biographical Introduction by J. C. Ryle (First published, without J. C. Ryle's Introduction, in three volumes, 1655,

1658, 1662; repr., Glasgow: Blackie and Son, 1864; repr., Edinburgh: Banner of Truth Trust, 1964).

8. John Trevor Cliffe addresses the role of Puritans in the seventeenth-century English wars in his recent book *Puritans in Conflict: The Puritan Gentry during and after the Civil Wars* (London: Routledge, 1988). Another recent book covers roughly the same ground, with special reference to the Puritans: Derek Hirst, *Authority and Conflict: England 1603–1658* (Edward Arnold: London, 1986), vol. 4 of A. G. Dickens and Norman Gash, eds., *The New History of England*.

9. Peter Lewis, *The Genius of Puritanism* (Haywards Heath, Sussex: Carey Publications, 1979), p. 143.

10. William Gouge, *The Whole Armour of God* (London: Printed by John Beale for John Grismond, 1627).

11. Hugh McKeon, *An Inquiry into the Birth-place, Parentage, Life, and Writings, of the Reverend William Gurnall, M.A.* (Woodbridge: J. Loder, 1830), pp. 1, 4.

12. I:xvii.

13. Ibid., p. xviii.

14. *Confession of Faith; the Larger and Shorter Catechisms, with the Scripture Proofs at Large; Together with the Sum of Saving Knowledge* (Glasgow: Free Presbyterian Publications, 1985), p. 14.

15. McKeon, *Inquiry into Gurnall*, p. 4.

16. I:xix.

17. Cliffe, *Puritans in Conflict*, p. 67. Cliffe remarks: 'In July 1643 Sir Simonds D'Ewes noted in his parliamentary journal that the House commonly dispensed with the presence of some thirty or forty MPs (out of a total of about 300) at any one time in order that "this bloody and unnatural civill Warre" could be carried on.'

18. I:xxiv.

19. Cliffe, *Puritans in Conflict*, p. 143.

20. McKeon, *Inquiry into Gurnall*, pp. 7–9.

21. Ibid., pp. 15, 16.
22. Edmund S. Morgan, *The Puritan Family* (New York: Harper and Row, 1966), pp. 29, 47, 52, 60–64.
23. I:xxxv.
24. Ibid., pp. xxxi, xxxii.
25. Quoted in ibid., p. xxxii. The language unmistakably refers to the Solemn League and Covenant, agreed upon by Parliament and the Westminster Assembly in 1643. The concern of the anonymous author is drawn especially from paragraph II: 'That we shall in like manner, without respect of persons, endeavour the extirpation of Popery, Prelacy, (that is, church-government by Archbishops, Bishops, their Chancellors, and Commissaries, Deans, Deans and Chapters, Archdeacons, and all other ecclesiastical Officers depending on that hierarchy,) superstition, heresy, schism, profaneness, and whatsoever shall be found to be contrary to sound doctrine and the power of godliness, lest we partake in other men's sins, and thereby be in danger to receive of their plagues; and that the Lord may be one, and his name one, in the three kingdoms' (*Confession of Faith*, p. 359).
26. I:xv.

Chapter 2   The Enemy

1. Paul Bayne, 'An Exposition of Ephesians, Chapter 2:11 to 6:18,' in *Puritan Exposition of Ephesians* (USA: Sovereign Grace Book Club, 1959), p. 603.
2. Gouge, p. 30.
3. This writer will not try to be perfectly consistent in the plural or singular use of 'devil'. The Puritans switch back and forth at will.
4. Perkins, *Witchcraft*, first and second pages of the Epistle Dedicatory.
5. G. E. Aylmer, *A Short History of Seventeenth-Century*

England (New York: The New American Library, Mentor Books, 1963), pp. 144–47.

6. William Perkins, *The Combat Between Christ and the Divell Displayed*, 2nd ed. (London: Melchisedech Bradwood, 1606), p. 41.

7. Brian Crozier, 'The New Nebuchadnezzar,' *National Review* 42:17 (September 3, 1990): p. 32.

8. Gouge, p. 30.

9. Thomas Watson also observes that the devil is a usurper and tyrant, his kingdom one of slavery. Thomas Watson, *Body of Divinity*, rev. ed. by George Rogers (London: Passmore and Alabaster, 1890; repr., Grand Rapids, Michigan: Baker Book House, 1979), pp. 443, 444.

10. John Owen, *Temptation and Sin* in *Works*, ed. W. H. Goold (repr. London: Banner of Truth, 1966), vol. 6, p. 166.

11. For the later Puritan contention that the devil does far more damage through socially 'legitimate' human instruments than through witches, see Chapter 3 under heading 'Vulnerability of Specific Persons'.

12. Perkins, *Witchcraft*, p. 6. Perkins says of the laws by which the devil runs his kingdom, 'And amongst them all, the precepts of Witchcraft are the very chiefe and most notorious. For by them especially he holds up his kingdome.'

13. Jeffrey Burton Russell, *Lucifer: The Devil in the Middle Ages* (Ithaca, New York: Cornell University Press, 1984), pp. 296, 298. Russell comments: 'Whether the accused witches ever believed or practiced the Satanism attributed to them or whether it was wholly projected upon them by their enemies, the conviction that Satanic witchcraft was real pervaded Western society for three centuries and provoked a persecution that killed as many as a hundred thousand victims and brought untold suffering and terror to millions.'

Russell's comment that satanic witchcraft was believed

to be real should be kept in mind, particularly since many of the historians of the period are uncritical materialists, and often exceedingly high-minded. C. S. Lewis notes that no great praise is due to modern people for not executing witches, since few believe that satanic witches exist. 'You would not call a man humane for ceasing to set mousetraps if he did so because he believed there were no mice in the house', from C. S. Lewis, *Mere Christianity* (London: Fontana Books, 1955), pp. 24, 25.

The resurgence of occultism in our time, and the reluctance and horror with which many folk are admitting that people can consciously choose an ethic of evil and harm to others, may give rise to a more balanced historiography when dealing with occult beliefs and practices in other times.

14. Gouge, p. 31.
15. *The Complete Works of Thomas Manton*, ed. Thomas Smith, vol. 1 (London: James Nisbet and Co., 1870), p. 304. Manton, close contemporary of Gurnall, agrees that the devil's principality is stolen; he is a usurper.
16. Gouge, p. 32.
17. Despite the seriousness with which the Puritans treat the devil and his works, theirs is no dualism, two equal principles, good and evil, battling for supremacy. God's sovereignty is unequivocally asserted. Perkins' early statement is programmatic in this regard: 'If any doe think it strange, that Satan should in this sort oppose himselfe to the kingdom of God . . . They must knowe, that this and all other evills come to passe even by the will of God, who hath justly permitted the same; to punish the wicked for their horrible sinnes . . . To avenge himselfe upon Man . . . who having the truth revealed unto him, will not believe or obey it . . .' (*Witchcraft*, seventh and eighth pages of Epistle Dedicatory).

Bayne concurs: 'That God's just disposition is such, that

for executing his spiritual judgments and curses on the wicked . . . some of them are in the earth, . . . for the devil is come down in great rage,' p. 604.

Gouge, p. 31, says 'their dominion is by God's permission, who in just judgment for punishment of the wicked, hath given liberty to the Divell, to exercise jurisdiction over them.'

All this harks back to the Puritans' great Reformed forebear, Calvin: 'In old times the Manichees misused this passage to prove their wild notion of two principles; . . . They supposed the devil to be . . . an antagonist god . . . whom the righteous God would not subdue without great exertion. For Paul does not ascribe to devils a principality, which they seize without the consent, and exercise against the opposition, of God, but one which, as Scripture everywhere teaches, God, in righteous vengeance, allows them against the wicked.' From *Calvin's Commentaries*, ed. D. W. Torrance, *The Epistles of Paul the Apostle to the Galatians, Ephesians, Philippians and Colossians*, trans. T. H. L. Parker (Edinburgh and London: Oliver and Boyd, 1965), p. 219.

18. Richard Gilpin, *Daemonologia Sacra; or, a Treatise of Satan's Temptations* (1677; new ed., Edinburgh: James Nichol, 1867), p. 16.

19. Manton, vol. 1, p. 259.

20. Perkins, *Witchcraft*, page eight of Epistle Dedicatory.

21. Ibid., page two of Epistle Dedicatory.

22. John Downame, *The Christian Warfare*, 2nd ed. (London: Printed by Felix Kyngston for Elizabeth Burby, 1608), p. 40. Perkins makes the same point: the devil is 'an ancient spirit, whose skil hath beene confirmed by experience of the course of nature, for the space almost of sixe thousand yeares. Hence he hath attained to the knowledge of many secrets.' *Witchcraft*, p. 19.

23. Downame, p. 25.

24. The same point regarding religious service to the devil was made in the discussion of principalities. Obviously the statement was somewhat hyperbolic, as the Puritans know that not all unregenerate humans are satanists in a specific sense. Nevertheless, it does make the point held strongly by Puritanism and early Christianity generally, that being outside of Christ places one at the service of the devil, and there is no real middle ground.

25. Perkins, *Witchcraft*, p. 20.

26. Ibid., p. 20.

27. Gouge, p. 35.

28. Gilpin, p. 15.

29. Keith Thomas, *Religion and the Decline of Magic* (New York: Charles Scribner's Sons, 1971), p. 25. Thomas remarks concerning the impact of Protestantism (pp. 75, 76): 'Protestantism thus presented itself as a deliberate attempt to take the magical elements out of religion, to eliminate the idea that the rituals of the Church had about them a mechanical efficacy, and to abandon the effort to endow physical objects with supernatural qualities by special formulae of consecration and exorcism.'

30. Downame, p. 24.

31. Milton, the 'Puritan poet', says the same. In *Paradise Lost*, Satan looks upon his gathered armies, the newly fallen angels:

    The fellows of his crime, the followers rather—
    Far other once beheld in bliss—condemned
    For ever now to have their lot in pain,
    Millions of spirits for his fault amerced
    Of heaven, and from eternal splendours flung
    For his revolt, . . .   (Book I; lines 606–11)

32. Downame, p. 24.

33. Whether this diabolical unity of purpose excludes all possibility of conflict amongst devils is a question the Puritans do not seem to address. One is reminded of C. S.

Lewis's portrayal of demonic lust in *Screwtape Letters* and other of his writings. The self-absorption of devils is shown to be literally all-consuming, like a vacuum, a vortex of emptiness of soul into which others are sucked. The Puritans do not say anything about such possiblities amongst the devils themselves.

34. These works are filled with descriptions of the paranormal, sometimes collected from people known personally to the authors. (One fascinating aspect of these works is that they display the difference among the Puritans regarding the possibility of the miraculous today. Perkins seems to hold to a 'cessationist' position; the miraculous age is limited to apostolic times. Yet he strongly believes in the devils' involvement in false signs and wonders. Baxter on the other hand, agreeing that Satan does counterfeit miracles, believes in the possibility of divine signs and wonders, and in fact recounts several events in his personal experience that sound very similar to some of the things spoken of today in the charismatic renewal.) The occult activity these Puritans report is largely pooh-poohed by materialist historians, but (1) is interesting from an historical perspective, and (2) is interesting to reconsider in light of the growing backlash against scientism, and the recognition of the existence of the spiritual realm (however undiscerningly that interest might be expressed).

35. Gouge, p. 33.

36. Perkins, *Witchcraft*, page two of Epistle Dedicatory.

37. This paragraph from Gouge (p. 35) shows the extent to which the Puritans believe the devil can act in the world: 'he can violently move the ayre, and cause thunder and lightning, yea, and extraordinary fire to falle downe; he can exceedingly trouble the Seas, and cause such waves and billowes to arise, as shall swallow up ships and men: he can cause waters to swell over the bankes, and so make great breaches. On earth he can cause earthquakes: he can throw

downe the strongest buildings, and roote up the best settled trees, and move all things: he can carry and hurry up and downe, even in the aire, the bodies of men and beasts . . .'

38. Ibid.

39. Perkins says the devil imitates God in order to make his own work more effectual. This shows again the Puritan view that Satan is like a parasite: he cannot do anything original, so he copies; he possesses nothing, so borrows. 'Furthermore, God hath revealed his will to the Patriarchs, Prophets, and Apostles, by familiar conference, by dreams, by inspiration, by Trances: In the same manner, Satan hath his Divinors, and Soothsayers, his Pythonisses, his Cassandraes, his Sibylles, to whome he maketh knowne things to come, by familiar presence, by dreams, etc.' *Witchcraft*, page four of Epistle Dedicatory.

40. The wizards to whom Gurnall makes reference seem to be those 'cunning folk'—'wise women' or 'cunning men'—practitioners of popular magic, diviners, folk healers. Interestingly, secular historians accept the widespread practice of such 'white magic' as historically factual. They recognize both the fact that such folk existed and that many people had recourse to them. See the chapter in Thomas, 'Cunning men and popular magic,' pp. 212–52.

But the same historians (and anthropologists) repudiate the possibility that there was such a thing as maleficent witchcraft. As Norman Cohn puts it, there is a 'fantasy . . . that there exists a category of human beings that is pledged to the service of Satan; a sect that worships Satan in secret conventicles and, on Satan's behalf, wages relentless war against Christendom and against individual Christians' (p. 3). Again: 'This sect was wholly imaginary . . . there was no sect of witches . . . they were not an organized body, they did not fly through the air, and they did not worship Satan' (p. 12). From Norman Cohn, 'The Myth of

Satan and his Human Servants,' in *Witchcraft Confessions and Accusations,* ed. Mary Douglas (London: Tavistock Publications, 1970).

41. Downame, pp. 27, 28.
42. William Gouge thirty years before Gurnall makes the same point using almost exactly the same divisions: 'The government of Devils is onely in this world, and over the men thereof. It can no further extend, than to the compasse of this inferiour world under Heaven; neither can it longer last than the time of this world.' Gouge, p. 37.
43. Ibid.
44. Downame, pp. 27, 67.
45. How does this square with the account in Job of Satan appearing before God? The Puritans are well aware of this Scripture, as has been noted. It actually makes their point. Whatever communication the devil has with God in the spiritual realm, and whatever action and influence Satan exercises, all have to do only with this world, as with Job. The Puritan point is that heaven proper—the presence of God with all the blessed angels and saints—is forever inaccessible to Satan, out of his reach.
46. Bayne, p. 611.
47. Gouge, p. 37.
48. Bayne, p. 611. Calvin had said the same: 'By "darkness", as is well known, he means unbelief and ignorance of God, with their consequences. As the whole world is covered with darkness, the devil is the prince of this world.' Calvin, p. 218.
49. Gilpin, p. 69.
50. Gouge, pp. 37, 38.
51. John Bunyan, *The Pilgrim's Progress* (Harmondsworth, Middlesex: Penguin Books, 1965), pp. 204, 205. Bunyan actually ends the first part of his book on this note: the final rejection of Ignorance, taken to hell from the very gates of heaven. It is certainly possible that Bunyan may

have had the benefit of reading Gurnall. Gurnall's book was published from 1655 to 1662; Part I of Bunyan's work was published in 1678, written after his second imprisonment in 1675 (from p. 28 of Wilbur Smith's biographical sketch of Bunyan in John Bunyan, *The Holy War* (Chicago: Moody Press, 1948)).

52. Stan Gooch, *Creatures from Inner Space* (London: Rider and Company, 1984), see Chapter 10, 'Discarnates?' pp. 122–135.

53. Gilpin, p. 50.

54. Gurnall's statement may be taken directly from Gouge, p. 39: 'Grosly doe they erre in the nature of Devils, who thinke, and teach, that they be nothing but bad qualities and evill affections, which arise from our flesh.' Gouge is also concerned to combat that view of devils that 'maketh them to be but fables.'

55. So much for this as a 'new', up-to-date, modern idea. Another 'new' idea, with ancient roots, as is often the case.

56. Edward Langton writes that Calvin earlier addressed the same view, refuting from Scripture 'those who say that good angels are nothing but good aspirations or movements which God produces in men; and that, on the other hand, the devils are merely evil affections which are suggested by our flesh.' Edward Langton, *Satan, a Portrait* (London: Skeffington and Son, 1945), p. 90.

57. Gouge, p. 40.

58. Ibid.

59. Downame, p. 25.

60. Gouge, p. 40. Gurnall agrees: 'But the devil's spirit is never cowed, nor he weary of doing mischief, though he hath never stood still since first he began his walk to and fro the world' (I:178).

61. This seems a bit of speculative theology. Whether the devils will be torturers, or subject to the same, in hell seems an open question. Revelation 19 and 20 seem to forecast

the same destination for wicked angels and wicked human beings, but as for their interaction there, if any, the Scripture does not comment.

62. Gouge, p. 40: 'they are not subject to death: from the beginning of the world they have assaulted man; and to the end of the world shall they continue: whereby they must needs gather much experience, which is a great disadvantage.'

Perkins refers to the devil's 'plots exquisitely contrived' and to his great 'policie and power, which Satan hath reserved unto himselfe even in the state of his Apostasie, improved by experience and instantly practised upon the sonnes of men.' *Witchcraft*, page two of Epistle Dedicatory.

63. Gouge, p. 41, says the devil is 'wholly and onely set upon mischiefe and wickednesse ... by nature he is most impure: no iot, no dramme of goodnesse in him.'

64. This 'falling into sin untempted' would be true of Satan himself; as far as those who fell with him, he may have acted as their seducer and tempter. This seems to be what Milton says; see note 31, this chapter.

65. Gouge, p. 41.

66. Ibid.

67. Bayne, p. 612.

68. Ibid., p. 613.

69. Gouge, p. 41.

70. Baxter, p. 5.

71. Watson, p. 586.

72. Downame, pp. 18, 19.

73. Ibid., p. 16.

74. *The Works of the Reverend William Bridge, M.A.*, vol. 1 (London: Thomas Tegg, 1845), p. 132. In 'The Soul's Conflict with Itself', Richard Sibbes speaks of the devil's malice to the saints, and his envy of their happy condition: 'By his envy and subtilty we were driven out of paradise at the first ... When Satan seeth a man strongly and comfortably walk

with God, he can not endure that a creature of meaner rank by creation than himself should enjoy such happiness . . . he follows them with all dejecting and uncomfortable temptations that he can.' *The Complete Works of Richard Sibbes, D.D.*, vol. 1 (Edinburgh: James Nichol, 1862; repr. Edinburgh: Banner of Truth, 1973), p. 134.

75. Bayne, p. 613.

76. Baxter, p. 5.

77. Gurnall seems to echo William Gouge again: 'Most interpreters so expound it, as if the place of the Divels were heere set downe, namely, the Aire, which is oft called Heaven which being so, hereby is implied, that they have very great advantage against us, by reason of the place where they are.' Thus, being above us, they can spy on us, and so forth. Gouge, p. 43.

78. Bayne, p. 613.

79. Calvin, p. 219.

80. Downame, p. 25.

81. Gouge, p. 43.

82. Gouge, p. 44.

Chapter 3   The Embattled Christian

1. *Confession*, VI:2–4.

2. The book entitled *Temptation and Sin* contains three of Owen's works on this topic: 'Mortification of Sin', 'Temptation', and 'Indwelling Sin'.

3. *Confession*, VI:5.

4. Thomas Watson comments helpfully on the remains of original sin within the regenerate, distilling the essence of the Puritan view: 'It is not perfectly cured in this life. Though grace does subdue sin, yet it does not wholly remove it . . . Though the Spirit be still weakening and hewing down sin in the godly, yet the stump of original sin is left. It is a sea that will not, in this life, be dried up.'

Explaining the biblical references regarding the crucifixion and death of indwelling sin (Romans 6:6), Watson says believers are dead as to the guilt and power of sin: 'the love of sin is crucified.' They are also dead legally: 'As a man that is sentenced to death is dead in law, so they are legally dead to sin. There is a sentence of death gone out against sin. It shall die, and drop into the grave; but at the present sin has its life lengthened out. Nothing but the death of the body can quite free us from the body of this death.' *Body of Divinity*, pp. 102, 103.

5. Bridge, p. 129.

6. Downame, p. 64.

7. Two of the earlier writers, Bayne and Downame, converge here. They point out that even the most exalted man that ever lived—Christ himself—was assaulted by Satan. If this be so, how much more likely that he will attack easier prey?

Bayne, p. 605: 'It must teach all of us who are weak in grace, of small growth, not to wonder if we be troubled: for if the green wood escape not, what, shall we, dry in comparison, be exempted?'

Downame, p. 26: 'If therefore he durst encounter the most valiant souldiers that ever fought the Lords battailes, yea if he durst set upon our Saviour Christ himselfe; then surely there is no doubt but that he hath courage enough to set upon us who are weaker and feeble, altogether unable in our selves to make resistance.'

Does Downame's reference to the devil's 'courage' negate the idea of his cowardice, so common to the Puritans? Not necessarily. 'Cowardice' in this context does not necessarily mean timidity. We usually think of a 'coward' as a timid soul who is afraid of his own shadow, a sort of Casper Milquetoast stereotype. It seems to me the Puritan idea is more like our idea of a bully, or a sadist; a strong and perverse individual who gets no greater pleasure than inflicting fear or pain on the weak. Certain modern dictators might fit this definition. Another analogy is the predatory male, who makes it his business to deflower as many virgins as he can, where sexual pleasure is almost beside the point. The pleasure for him consists not so much in the physical pleasure he has received, as the fact that he has permanently soiled another human being.

8. Bayne, p. 608. Again note the sexual metaphor, the devil impregnating the fallen human, sin being the product. The Puritans sometimes use sexual imagery and to great effect. Milton says something similar to this in *Paradise Lost*, regarding the entrance of sin and death into the universe. In Satan's rebellion, Milton depicts Sin as a goddess, springing from the angel's head; she later reminds him

> Thyself in me thy perfect image viewing,
> Became enamoured, and such joy thou took'st
> With me in secret, that my womb conceived
> A growing burden. . . .
> Pregnant by thee, and now excessive grown,
> Prodigious motion felt, and rueful throes.
> At last this odious offspring whom thou seest,
> Thine own begotten, breaking violent way, . . .
> Forth issued, brandishing his fatal dart,
> Made to destroy. I fled, and cried out Death!'
> (Book II; lines 764–67, 779–82, 786, 787)

In this Milton is consistent with the common practice of the Puritan preachers.

9. Baxter, page nine of Preface.

10. Downame, p. 71.

11. It is helpful to remember that Puritan teaching usually takes place in the setting of a sermon. *The Christian in Complete Armour* is several years' worth of preaching— Gurnall addressing 'the Christian' in the context of the gathered community at Lavenham.

12. Richard Baxter, with his characteristic largeness of vision,

speaks to the saints regarding the fact that the Christian warfare is not to be left only to professional ministers. All the saints are to engage themselves, for themselves, for each other, and for the world at large: 'O! do not say as Cain, Am I my Brothers Keeper, say not, that it is only the Work of Ministers: They are Guides in Christs Army, but you are Souldiers: You are Vowed to fight against the Devil, the World and Flesh, and that for others, as well as for yourselves: Societies are for Mutual Helps. A Minister is but one Man, and not an Army, and can be but in one place at once: You live among and near your Family, Neighbours and such as you Converse with, and may often speak to them: All in your places must be Light and Salt, to Enlighten a Dark, and season a Corrupt Generation.' Baxter, pp. 12, 13.

13. Watson, p. 589. Bayne strikes the same note: 'Generally, his policy in fight is, that he observeth all circumstances for his advantage, as person, place, time; . . . The condition of the party . . . , his weapon, in choosing and using of which he hath great skill'. Bayne, p. 595.

14. Downame, p. 93.

15. Watson begins at conversion as well: 'He tempts us in our first initiation and entrance into religion, when we have newly given up our names to Christ.' Watson, p. 589.

16. Downame, p. 84.

17. Ibid.

18. Owen, pp. 127, 128.

19. Watson, pp. 531, 532.

20. Downame, p. 78. Notice that Downame explicitly mentions the supposed linkage between wealth and God's favour, and denies it legitimacy, saying such a view is of the devil. Indeed, Owen warns that prosperity, without special grace, has 'an inconceivably malignant influence on believers themselves.' He calls delight and satisfaction in creature-comforts 'the poison of the soul.' Owen, pp. 127, 128.

21. Gilpin, p. 38.
22. Downame, p. 79. Downame notes that people who have been robbed, or have otherwise lost material possessions, are tempted by the devil 'to goe to witches and wizards, that so we may hazard our soules, which are of more value than the whole world, for the recoverie of some earthly trifle.' An interesting parallel in our own time is the phone-in radio show, featuring a psychic who will advise callers on where to find lost articles and so on. A pastor from India, known to this writer, before his conversion was a trained astrologer. He said that many of his Canadian clients were professing Christians.
23. Gurnall's statement is later borrowed by Watson, with very little change: 'when provisions grow short, Satan sets in with a temptation; What, wilt thou starve rather than steal? reach forth thy hand, and pluck the forbidden fruit.' Watson, p. 589.
24. Bunyan, pp. 198, 199.
25. Ibid., p. 199.
26. Watson, p. 590. Gurnall also contends that the devil puts forth his greatest effort when the saint is dying: 'As they say of the natural serpent, he never is seen at his length till dying; so this mystical serpent never strains his wit and wiles more, than when his time is thus short' (I:74).

    In Thomas Manton's 'Sermon upon Genesis 3:15', Manton asserts the same regarding the death of Christ: 'In his whole life he endured many outward troubles from Satan's instruments; for his life long he was a man of sorrows, wounded and bruised by Satan and his instruments: . . . But the closing stroke was at last; then did the serpent most eminently bruise his heel.' *The Complete Works of Thomas Manton, D.D.*, vol. 17 (London: James Nisbet and Company, 1874), pp. 248, 249.
27. Gilpin, p. 223.
28. Watson, p. 589. Baxter says this regarding the danger of

idleness, of time frivolously spent: 'If the Devil can get People (perhaps Lords and Ladies) to spend the Day (their precious Hours) in Cards and Dice, and Feastings, and Stage-Plays, and Masks and Musick, and perhaps filthy Lust, he will let you say your Prayers at Night, and cry God Mercy, and perhaps tell him that you Repent, that you may sin on the more boldly the next day'. Baxter, pp. 224, 225.

29. Bayne, p. 596.

30. Watson, p. 589.

31. Owen, p. 129. Instead of Peter, Owen uses the example of Paul, referring to Paul's exalted experiences (recorded in 2 Corinthians 12:7), instantly followed by satanic attack. Owen warns that overpowering experiences of the love of God should not blind the saint to the presence of the enemy.

32. 'Master' Perkins early on speaks to this in his commentary on the temptation of Christ. Speaking concerning Jesus' 'solemne inauguration into his mediatorship', and how soon after this he was exposed to temptation, 'we learn, that all those that are set apart by God to any speciall calling, even at their verie entrance thereinto must looke for temptations.' Perkins, *Combat*, p. 2.

33. Baxter, p. 244. Watson remarks that the devil 'makes use of such as are in places of dignity, men of renown. He knows, if he can get these on his side, they may draw others into snares.' Watson, p. 596.

34. Baxter, p. 246. Notice again the Puritan balance and emphasis: the acceptance of witchcraft as a real factor, but also not the most important. Satan is seen working far more through the normal and 'legitimate' organs of society than through various occultists. This statement by Baxter, amongst the later Puritans, seems to represent a change from Perkins, who placed such strong emphasis on witchcraft and the influence of witches.

35. This insight of Gurnall's is echoed by a modern theologian and Puritan scholar, who makes a remarkably similar point about the duties of a theologian: 'So one who theologizes in public, whether formally in the pulpit, on the podium or in print, or informally from the armchair, must think hard about the effect his thoughts will have on people—God's people, and other people. Theologians are called to be the church's water engineers and sewage officers; it is their job to see that God's pure truth flows abundantly where it is needed, and to filter out any intrusive pollution that might damage health.' From James I. Packer, *A Quest for Godliness: The Puritan Vision of the Christian Life* (Wheaton, Illinois: Crossway Books, 1990), p. 15.

36. Gouge, p. 27. John Downame also addresses this issue as a contemporary problem, stating in the strongest terms the trouble that is caused in the church by unfaithful leadership: 'And thus now adaies he useth professors, yea preachers of the Gospell, as meanes to tempt men to sinne, both by their words and evill examples: which temptation is farre more dangerous and of greater force, then if all worldlings should combine themselves together'. Downame, p. 101. Downame's warning that the greatest danger to the church is from within seems a perennially valuable piece of wisdom.

37. Downame, p. 101. This is a remarkable insight for a somewhat top-heavy Christian movement. The Puritan sense, both of the importance of leadership, yet of their own vulnerability, shows a balance that is not always present in church leaders.

38. This quote is from Brooks' famous work *Precious Remedies Against Satan's Devices*, in *The Complete Works of Thomas Brooks*, vol. 1 (Edinburgh: James Nichol, 1866; repr. Edinburgh: Banner of Truth, 1980), p. 125.

39. Watson, p. 597. This is very similar to Gurnall's statement,

that the instruments used by the devil are 'commonly subtle-pated men' (I:80).

40. Watson, p. 598.

41. Brooks, p. 125.

42. Watson again nearly quotes William Gurnall verbatim: the flesh 'will not endure any yoke, unless it be lined and made soft.' Watson, p. 598.

43. Downame, p. 86. Downame makes clear these are not just 'apparent' Christians, but truly mature believers, the devil's work being to distort their Christian lives, to elevate a lesser good over a greater, to put virtues in conflict, to make worship valueless, to render them ineffective, or worse.

44. Gurnall gives a striking illustration of the temptation for holy persons to be their own bad examples: 'Now a soul that rests on any holiness in himself, he grafts his comfort upon himself, not upon Christ; he sucks his own breast, not Christ's, and so makes Christ a dry nurse; and what comfort can grow on that dry tree?' (I:208).

45. John Downame writes that the devil makes use 'of our deare friends and acquaintance and our neere kindred; sometime our brother or sister, our parents and children, yea sometimes a mans wife which lieth in his bosome, plaieth the part of the tempter.' As biblical examples he mentions Job's wife, Eve, and Jezebel. Downame, p. 100.

46. Bunyan, pp. 40, 41.

47. Downame, p. 100.

48. Bunyan, p. 149.

Chapter 4   The Christian's Battlegear

1. Bayne, p. 594.

2. Bunyan, p. 90. John Downame long before said, 'There is not any peece appointed for the backe, to note unto us that we must never retire, but manfully stand to it even in the

face of our enemie. For if we resist Satan, he will flee from us, James 4:7, . . . neither will the Lord protect such faint-hearted cowards as runne away from his standard, not daring to trust and relie upon his almightie power . . . , which he hath promised to all that fight his battles' (pp. 71, 72).

3. Ibid., pp. 175, 176.

4. Gouge, p. 26.

5. The Puritans' confidence in the omnipotence of God gives them assurance of final victory in spiritual warfare: 'For our comfort, note, that though wrestling imply a sore combate, yet it implieth not a conquest over us: of this there is no feare: for Christ our head hath overcome our enemie, . . . Though they be spirits, yet God (in the power of whose might we are strong) is a Spirit of spirits, the highest Spirit, every way infinite. God is invisible even to them, and they are blinde as Beetles to God: they cannot know the counsell of God, yet God knoweth all their devices; . . . he discovereth all the purposes of the wicked one, and thrusteth him out of his hold'. Gouge, pp. 26, 40.

6. Ibid., p. 13.

7. Downame, p. 49.

8. Gouge, p. 62.

9. Gurnall's quite technical sounding definition (technical not in a negative sense, but meaning theologically precise) is actually lifted almost verbatim from William Gouge's exposition of the breastplate: 'This righteousnesse is a powerful work of God's Spirit in the regenerate, whereby they endevour to approve themselves unto God and man, by performing what God's Law requireth to be performed unto both.' Gouge, p. 72.

Bayne, p. 626, sees the breastplate as 'righteousness of the course and conversation'; Downame, p. 51, says it is a 'good conscience, true sanctification, and a godly life.'

Henry's comment is, 'The righteousness of Christ implanted in us is our breastplate' from Matthew Henry's *Commentary on the Whole Bible*, vol. 6, Acts to Revelation (Scottsdale, Pennsylvania: Herald Press, 1970), p. 720.

The Puritans here echo Calvin: 'Some imagine that this refers to free righteousness, or the imputation of righteousness, which consists of remission of sins. But to my mind this would be irrelevant here; for Paul is dealing with innocence of life. He wants us to be adorned, first, with integrity, and next with a devout and holy life.' Calvin, p. 220.

10. Gouge, p. 72.
11. Downame, p. 52.
12. Bayne, p. 626.
13. Downame, p. 52. Gouge also uses 'endeavour': 'Righteousnesse is . . . an holy quality wrought in us by God's Spirit, whereby we endeavour to square and frame all our thoughts, words, and actions, unto the righteous rule of the Law of God.' Gouge, p. 71.
14. Bunyan, p. 93.
15. Downame, p. 52.
16. This writer can speak to the point with some experience. He still possesses—and uses—a pair of combat boots from his time in the United States Army, 1972–1975. Durability!
17. Calvin, p. 220. Notice how John Downame takes this basic conception and fleshes it out. He says that Paul 'alludeth to the custome of souldiers in former times, who going into the field, strongly armed their legges and feete with legge-harnesse, wargraves or buskins, to preserve them from the injurie of the weather, the piercing of briars, thornes, and such other things as might hurt them in their way as they marched, and from the violence also of their enemies blowes when they were encountred; for all which uses the

Gospell serveth in our spirituall warfare: for they who are armed with the true knowledge thereof, and are assured of the merciful promises therein contained, they will walk and march valiantly in the waies of godliness . . . though they are ful of the briars and thornes of afflictions and persecution.' Downame, p. 54.

18. Bayne, p. 630.

19. Sibbes, p. cv. Quotations could be multiplied on this score: Matthew Poole comments on the fact that the apostle prefaces his remarks on the shield of faith by saying 'Above all': 'this he sets, as the principal part of the Christian'. Matthew Poole, *A Commentary on the Whole Bible*, vol. 3, Matthew–Revelation (First ed. pub. 1685; repr., London: Banner of Truth Trust, 1963), p. 679.

   Likewise in Matthew Henry, p. 720: 'This is more necessary than any of them. Faith is all in all to us in an hour of temptation.'

20. Gurnall says that love will be the end; in heaven, it will possess the inheritance, but on earth faith is that which first unites the soul to Christ (II:12). This idea may be an echo of a comment by Sibbes, who notes the pre-eminence of faith now: 'until that blessed time when we shall be put into a full possession of all things we have now only in promise, when faith shall end in fruition, and promises in performance.' Sibbes, p. cv. This sounds a little like the faith a betrothed couple exercise in one another, until their wedding brings fruition and full expression of love to their mutual trust.

21. Poole, p. 679. Manton, vol. 1, p. 228, says: 'A shield covers the body, but that which gives defence to all is faith: without this a man is naked. Destitute of Christ's imputed righteousness, he wants his covenant strength.'

22. This quote, though from a modern scholar, fits well with the Puritan idea of faith. Merrill C. Tenney, ed. *The Zondervan Pictorial Encyclopedia of the Bible*, vol. 2

(Grand Rapids, Michigan: Zondervan, 1978), s.v. 'Faith, faithfulness' by R. E. Nixon, p. 490.

23. Watson, pp. 350, 351.

24. Ibid., p. 352.

25. 'Faith believes that God will provide; that he who feeds the birds will feed his children; that he who clothes the lilies will clothe his lambs; and thus faith overcomes the world. Faith is the cure of care.' Ibid.

26. Poole, p. 932.

27. Brooks, p. 68. Brooks shows that the possession of worldly honors is cold comfort when death comes calling: 'Is it honours, riches, or friends, etc., that can comfort thee when thou comest to die? Or is it not rather faith in the blood of Christ, the witness of the Spirit of Christ, the sense and feeling of the love and favour of Christ, and the hopes of eternally reigning with Christ?' p. 69.

28. Bayne concurs, p. 647. So also Downame, p. 57. Poole also sees the helmet as hope, p. 679, as does Henry, p. 720. And so on.

29. Downame, p. 58.

30. Paul Bayne, p. 647, had described hope similarly: 'And it may be described, a certain expecting to attain everything faith believeth, grounded only on God's grace.'

31. Downame, p. 58.

32. Bayne, p. 647.

33. Other Puritans also show that this hope encourages the despairing: Henry notes that Satan tempts to despair, 'but good hope keeps us trusting in God, and rejoicing in him', p. 720. Hope returns to the pilgrims when, imprisoned by Giant Despair, they find the Key of Promise, which enables them to escape Doubting Castle. Bunyan, p. 156.

34. Downame, p. 58. Gurnall makes exactly the same point in demonstrating the usefulness of the helmet. Hope 'ennobles and enables the Christian to contemn the present world, with all its pomp, treasure, and pleasure, to which

the rest of the sons of men are, every man of them, basely enslaved and held by the leg as a prisoner by his chain' (II:136).

35. Marshall Mason Knappen, *Tudor Puritanism: A Chapter in the History of Idealism* (Chicago: University of Chicago Press, 1939; Phoenix Books, 1965), pp. 354, 365. Knappen contends the Puritans held a very wooden view of Scripture, that in all but name they 'held the dictation theory of inspiration', p. 357. 'True, human hands held the pens, but the mortals were only amanuenses', p. 356. He says the Puritans nearly treated the Bible as a magical charm, p. 365.

These contentions seem wrong on all counts. What is clear when reading the Puritans is how seriously they engage with the text, both Old and New Testaments, not as a magically effective rabbit's foot (as already pointed out, they emphatically reject both Catholic and Protestant mechanical/magical religion), but as contentful speech by, about, and from God, through human beings. They often interact with the human writers as the writers of Scripture, but always with the understanding that God is the primary Author. When the Puritans use the language of dictation, it is hyperbolic, meant to make the point that God is indeed the Author. But they never treat the human writers as robots, or the Scriptures as the product of automatic writing.

What Knappen and many others find impossible to accept, the Puritans assert: the Bible is both fully from God, and fully the product of its human writers. Knappen says these cancel each other out; the Puritans say, no, they are both true simultaneously.

36. *Confession*, p. 19.

37. Watson, p. 20. Downame holds the same view, pp. 59, 60. So with Poole, p. 679; Henry, p. 720; Gilpin, p. 465.

38. Bayne, p. 653.

39. *Works of John Owen*, vol. 4 (Banner of Truth Trust, 1967), p. 14.

40. Henry affirms Gurnall's statement: 'the sword of the Spirit, . . . is of the Spirit's inditing and he renders it efficacious and powerful', p. 720.

41. Calvin, p. 221.

42. Perkins, *Combat*, p. 19. The dual defensive/offensive nature of this weapon is also found in Bayne, p. 653: 'it is either defensive, warding the blows which Satan doth reach us . . . , or offensive, it doth strike down the darkness and power of sin in us.' Thomas Manton, vol. 1, p. 228, writes, 'Then there is "the sword of the Spirit," which is both offensive and defensive; it wardeth off Satan's blows, and makes him fly back from us as one wounded and ashamed.' Richard Gilpin, p. 467, comments: 'whereas other parts of the armour are defensive, this of the Scripture is compared to the sword, which not only defends, but also offends and beats back the enemy.'

43. Bunyan, p. 94. That the sword is the Word of God is made very plain. As he strikes Apollyon, Christian quotes the Scripture, and later in the passage Bunyan remarks that Christian 'perceived he had wounded Apollyon with his two-edged sword', a clear allusion to Hebrews 4:12.

44. Calvin, p. 221.

45. Thomas, p. 68. The observations noted here, under discussion of the Word of God, reprise similar matters found in Chapter 2 under Powers. See Chapter 2, Note 29.

46. Perkins, *Combat*, p. 19.

47. Downame, p. 63. So with Bayne, who criticizes both Catholic emphasis on church tradition, and their withholding of the Scriptures: 'Which doth first let us see the lewdness of the papists; . . . they give us a leaden sword, . . . , the word of men, as well as of God. The mixture doth mar the metal; but above all, herein they sin, that they let not Christians indifferently have the word of God in their

mother tongue; . . . And mark it, for this taking the word from God's people is an antichristian practice', p. 656.

48. C. S. Lewis, p. 71, writing to a slightly different issue, nevertheless makes the Puritan point: 'The proper motto is not "Be good, sweet maid, and let who can be clever", but "Be good, sweet maid, and don't forget that this involves being as clever as you can."'

Downame, p. 62, points out the need for skill, and thus the need, not for a skilled élite to rule the ignorant, but for a continuous coming to the Word of God to become skilled. The Puritans do not believe in a spiritual welfare state, wherein the needy are served by a bureaucracy that keeps them needy—and in continuing need of the bureaucracy. As the saying goes, 'If you give a hungry man a fish, he will soon be hungry again. Teach him how to fish, and he can catch his own.' The Puritans would agree.

In fact Peter Lewis, p. 59, records a story told by George Swinnock that makes exactly the same point: '"I have read a story," he writes, "of two men who, walking together, found a young tree laden with fruit. They both gathered and satisfied themselves at present; one of them took all the remaining fruit and carried it away with him; the other took the tree, and planted it in his own ground where it prospered and brought forth fruit every year, so that though the former had more at present, yet this had some when he had none. Those who hear the word and have large memories and nothing else, may carry most of the word at present, yet, he that possibly can remember little who carries away the tree, plants the word in his heart and obeys it in his life, shall have fruit when the other hath none."'

49. Henry, p. 720. Downame, p. 62, says we must have the sword ready for combat 'that we may strike home, and cut off . . . the lusts of our owne flesh when they doe assault us.'

50. Gouge, p. 2.

51. Downame, pp. 63, 64.
52. Henry, p. 720.
53. Owen, vol. 4, p. 297.
54. Henry, p. 721.
55. Bayne, p. 659.
56. Owen, vol. 4, p. 330.
57. Ibid., p. 331.
58. Bayne, p. 659.
59. Ibid.
60. Henry, p. 720.
61. Ibid.
62. Owen, vol. 4, pp. 298, 299. Owen comments that most believers have at one time or another been in such a condition.

Chapter 5   Conclusion

1. William Haller, *The Rise of Puritanism* (Columbia University Press, 1938; repr. Philadelphia: University of Pennsylvania Press, 1972), pp. 85, 86.

Bibliography

Aylmer, G. E. *A Short History of Seventeenth-Century England.* New York: The New American Library, Mentor Books, 1963.

Baxter, Richard. *The Certainty of the Worlds of Spirits.* London: T. Parkhurst and I. Salusbury, 1691.

Bayne, Paul. 'An Exposition of Ephesians, Chapter 2:11 to 6:18.' In *Puritan Exposition of Ephesians.* Evansville, Indiana: Sovereign Grace Book Club, 1959.

Bridge, William. *The Works of the Reverend William Bridge, M.A.* Vol. 1. London: Thomas Tegg, 1845.

Brooks, Thomas. *The Complete Works of Thomas Brooks.* Edinburgh: James Nichol, 1861–67; repr., Edinburgh: Banner of Truth, 1980. Vol. 1.

Bunyan, John. *The Holy War.* With a biographical sketch, introduction, and notes by Wilbur M. Smith. Chicago: Moody Press, 1948.

—. *The Pilgrim's Progress.* Harmondsworth, Middlesex: Penguin Books Ltd., 1965.

Calvin, John. *Calvin's Commentaries.* Edited by D. W. Torrance. The Epistles of Paul the Apostle to the Galatians, Ephesians, Philippians and Colossians. Translated by T. H. L. Parker. Edinburgh and London: Oliver and Boyd, 1965.

Cliffe, John Trevor. *Puritans in Conflict: the Puritan Gentry during and after the Civil Wars.* London: Routledge, 1988.

Cohn, Norman. 'The Myth of Satan and his Human Servants.' In Mary Douglas, ed., *Witchcraft Confessions and Accusations*, pp. 3–16. London: Tavistock Publications, 1970.

Confession of Faith; the Larger and Shorter Catechisms, with the Scripture Proofs at Large; Together with the Sum of Saving Knowledge. Glasgow: Free Presbyterian Publications, 1985.

Cramer, Marc. *The Devil Within.* London: W. H. Allen, 1980.

Crozier, Brian. 'The New Nebuchadnezzar.' *National Review* 42:17 (September 3, 1990): 32.

Downame, John. *The Christian Warfare.* 2nd ed. London: Printed by Felix Kyngston for Elizabeth Burby, 1608.

Fisher, Joe. *Hungry Ghosts: An Investigation into Channeling and the Spirit World.* Toronto: Doubleday Canada, 1990.

Forsyth, Neil. *The Old Enemy: Satan and the Combat Myth.* Princeton, New Jersey: Princeton University Press, 1987.

Frye, Roland Mushat. *God, Man, and Satan: Patterns of Christian Thought and Life in Paradise Lost, Pilgrim's Progress, and the Great Theologians.* Princeton, New Jersey: Princeton University Press, 1960.

Gilpin, Richard. *Daemonologia Sacra; or, a Treatise of Satan's Temptations.* 1677; new ed., Edinburgh: James Nichol, 1867.

Gooch, Stan. *Creatures from Inner Space.* London: Rider and Company, 1984.

Goodman, Felicitas D. 'How About Demons? Possession and Exorcism in the Modern World.' In Linda Degh, ed., *Folklore Today.* Bloomington and Indianapolis: Indiana University Press, 1988.

Goodwin, Thomas. *The Works of Thomas Goodwin.* Edinburgh: James Nichol, 1861–65. Vols. 3, 5, 7.

Gouge, William. *The Whole Armour of God.* London: Printed by John Beale for John Grismond, 1627.

Gurnall, William. *The Christian in Complete Armour.* With a Biographical Introduction by J. C. Ryle. Glasgow: Blackie and Son, 1864; repr., London: The Banner of Truth Trust, 1964.

Haller, William. *The Rise of Puritanism.* Columbia University, 1938; repr., Philadelphia: University of Pennsylvania Press, 1972.

Henry, Matthew. *Matthew Henry's Commentary.* Vol. 6. Acts to Revelation. Scottsdale, Pennsylvania: Herald Press, 1970.

Hirst, Derek. *Authority and Conflict: England 1603–1658,* vol. 4 of A. G. Dickens and Norman Gash, eds., *The New History of England.* London: Edward Arnold, 1986.

Knappen, Marshall Mason. *Tudor Puritanism: A Chapter in the History of Idealism.* Chicago: University of Chicago Press, 1939; repr., Phoenix Books, 1965.

Langton, Edward. *Essentials of Demonology: A Study of Jewish and Christian Doctrine, its Origin and Development.* London: Epworth Press, 1949; repr., New York: AMS Press, 1982.

—. *Satan, a Portrait.* London: Skeffington, 1945.

Lewis, C. S. *The Discarded Image: An Introduction to Medieval and Renaissance Literature.* Cambridge: Cambridge University Press, 1964.

—. *Mere Christianity.* London: Fontana Books, 1955.

—. *Studies in Medieval and Renaissance Literature.* Cambridge: Cambridge University Press, 1966.

Lewis, Peter. *The Genius of Puritanism*. Haywards Heath, Sussex: Carey Publications, 1979.

Lieb, Michael. *Poetics of the Holy: A Reading of Paradise Lost*. Chapel Hill, North Carolina: University of North Carolina Press, 1981.

Lloyd-Jones, D. M. *The Christian Soldier: An Exposition of Ephesians 6:10 to 20*. Edinburgh: Banner of Truth Trust, 1977.

—. *The Christian Warfare: An Exposition of Ephesians 6:10 to 13*. Edinburgh: Banner of Truth Trust, 1976.

—. *The Puritans: Their Origins and Successors*. Edinburgh: Banner of Truth Trust, 1987.

Macfarlane, Alan. *Witchcraft in Tudor and Stuart England*. London: Routledge and Kegan Paul, 1970.

McKeon, Hugh. *An Inquiry into the Birth-place, Parentage, Life, and Writings, of the Reverend William Gurnall, M.A.* Woodbridge: Printed and Published by J. Loder, for the author, 1830.

—. *An Inquiry into the Rights of the Poor, of the Parish of Lavenham, in Suffolk, with Historical Notes and Observations*. London: Printed for Baldwin and Cradock, 1829.

Manton, Thomas. *The Complete Works of Thomas Manton, D.D.* Vol. 1. London: James Nisbet and Company, 1870–75. Vols. 1, 17.

Mather, Cotton. *The Wonders of the Invisible World*. London: John Dunton at the Raven in the Poultry, 1693; repr., London: John Russell Smith, 1862.

Morgan, Edmund. *The Puritan Family*. New York: Harper and Row, 1966.

Nixon, R. E. 'Fear, faithfulness.' In Merrill C. Tenney, ed., *The

Zondervan Pictorial Encyclopedia of the Bible, vol. 2. Grand Rapids, Michigan: Zondervan, 1978.

Notestein, Wallace. *A History of Witchcraft in England from 1558 to 1718.* Washington, D.C.: The American Historical Association, 1911; reissued, New York: Russell and Russell, 1965.

O'Grady, Joan. *The Prince of Darkness: The Devil in History, Religion and the Human Psyche.* Great Britain: Element Books Ltd., 1989.

Owen, John. *The Works of John Owen.* Johnstone and Hunter, 1850–53; repr., London: Banner of Truth Trust, 1965–68. Vols. 4, 6.

Packer, James I. *A Quest for Godliness: The Puritan Vision of the Christian Life.* Wheaton, Illinois: Crossway Books, 1990.

Perkins, William. *The Combat Between Christ and The Divell Displayed.* 2nd ed. London: Melchisedech Bradwood, 1606.

—. *A Discourse of the Damned Art of Witchcraft.* Cambridge: Published by Thomas Pickering, printed by Cantrel Legge, 1610.

Poole, Matthew. *A Commentary on the Whole Bible.* Vol. 3, Matthew–Revelation. 1685; repr., London: Banner of Truth Trust, 1963.

Raschke, Carl. *Painted Black.* San Francisco: Harper and Row, 1990.

Rougemont, Denis de. *The Devil's Share.* Translated by Haakon Chevalier. New York: Bollingen Foundation Inc., Pantheon Books, 1946.

Russell, Jeffrey Burton. *The Devil: Perceptions of Evil from Antiquity to Primitive Christianity.* Ithaca, New York: Cornell University Press, 1977.

—. *A History of Witchcraft: Sorcerers, Heretics, and Pagans.* London: Thames and Hudson, 1980.

—. *Lucifer: The Devil in the Middle Ages.* Ithaca, New York: Cornell University Press, 1984.

—. *Mephistopheles: The Devil in the Modern World.* Ithaca, New York: Cornell University Press, 1986.

—. *The Prince of Darkness: Radical Evil and the Power of Good in History.* Ithaca, New York: Cornell University Press, 1988.

—. *Satan.* London: Sheed and Ward, 1951.

Scot, Reginald. *The Discoverie of Witchcraft.* 1584; repr., Carbondale, Illinois: Southern Illinois University Press, Centaur Press, 1964.

Sibbes, Richard. *The Complete Works of Richard Sibbes, D.D.* Edinburgh: James Nichol, 1862–64; repr., Edinburgh: Banner of Truth Trust, 1973–82. Vol. 1.

Thomas, Keith. *Religion and the Decline of Magic.* New York: Charles Scribner's Sons, 1971.

Twelftree, Graham H. *Christ Triumphant: Exorcism Then and Now.* London: Hodder and Stoughton, 1985.

Watson, Thomas. *Body of Divinity.* Revised by George Rogers. London: Passmore and Alabaster, 1890; repr., Grand Rapids, Michigan: Baker Book House, 1979.

Weisman, Richard. *Witchcraft, Magic, and Religion in 17th-Century Massachusetts.* Massachusetts: University of Massachusetts Press, 1984.

Weyer, Johann. *De praestigiis daemonum,* translated by John Shea, edited by George Mora as *Witches, Devils, and Doctors in the Renaissance.* Binghamton, New York: Medieval and Renaissance Texts and Studies, vol. 73, 1991.